About the author

William James Roop, M.A.B.S., has been an Associate Pastor at Pentecostal Deliverance Church in Lafayette, LA., Adjunct Professor at Apostolic Theological Seminary, Missionary to Guatemala and Pakistan, Hospice Volunteer, Church Historian, Church Librarian, and much more. He has authored four books, one Bible Study, and has three YouTube channels, and three blogs. He is married to Gretchen Roop-Crappell, a former missionary to Guatemala and France.

Book: The Basics of Biblical Hermeneutics.

Book: Love without Limits.

Book: Apostolic Church History, Volume 1.

Book: Apostolic Church History, Volume 2.

Bible Study: The 3 R's of Salvation.

YouTube Channel: Brother Roop teaches the Bible.

YouTube Channel: Brother Roop.

YouTube Channel: Bill & Gretchen's Tin Can.

Blog: The Bible and Life.

Blog: Hospice Care and Dying.

Blog: The Trucking Tango.

Email: roopwilliam@yahoo.com

Website: www.billroopministries.com

THE BASICS OF BIBLICAL HERMENEUTICS

BY
WILLIAM JAMES ROOP, M.A.B.S.
April 2019

The Basics
Of
Biblical Hermeneutics

Edited by

Bernadine Rose Roop

Table of Contents

All images are courtesy of Google Creative Commons

Forward

What is the Bible, who wrote it, and what good is it? That's a very good question and it was answered by the Apostle Paul two-thousand years ago to Timothy, a young minister. "All scripture is given by inspiration of God and is profitable for doctrine, for reproof, for correction, for instruction in righteousness." 2 Timothy 3:16.

By God giving His Word to men, through inspiration, to be copied down and preached to the world, it is the Word of God! The writer of the book of Hebrews understood that it is the Word of God. "For the Word of God is quick, and powerful, and sharper than any two-edged sword, piercing even to the dividing asunder of soul and spirit, and the joints and marrow, and is a discerner of the thoughts and intents of the heart." Hebrews 4:12.

The Word of God was inspired by the Spirit of God in the lives of chosen men to write or speak that inspiration. God always has a desire to work His Will through His creation. This includes mankind. The Apostle Peter explained it in his second letter. "For the prophecy came not in old time by the will of man; but holy men of God spoke as they were moved by the Holy Ghost." 2 Peter 1:21.

Because God was giving these me divine inspiration, they wrote and spoke things that they did not understand. The prophet, and king, David wrote, 'The Spirit of the Lord spoke by me, and his word was in my tongue." 2 Samuel 23:2.

Here are some proofs that God's Spirit is proving inspiration and providence for His Word. First is the Bible's preeminence in world literature. The Bible is, and always has been, the number one book in print.

Second is the Bible's preservation throughout time. God has preserved His Word through wars, revolutions, captivity, natural disasters, hostile religions, and even exterminations. Through it all the Bible is still the most widespread book. Even when most other ancient writings have been lost to history.

Third, we can see the awe-inspiring transforming power of the Word of God. We can see this transforming power in people's lives in the history of the people in the Bible. We can see this transforming power in the lives of people in the world who have experienced a life changing conversion to Christianity, just by hearing the Word. "So then faith cometh by hearing, and hearing by the word of God." Romans 10:17. All of this by the working of the Spirit of God.

Fourth, the Bible's unity throughout human history attest to the divine inspiration of the Word of God. The Bible writers compiled the sacred book until the end of the Apostles ministry. Then it was canonized as a complete work. Since the time of the Apostles, the Bible has not changed, other than minor translational changes. The Aramaic Peshitta, the Bible of the east, has never been translated more than once, and so does not have those issues. The Bible's unity and perseveration for the last turbulent two thousand years attests to the divine authorship and protection.

Fifth, the scientific accuracy of the Bible makes the book stand out as a divine writing. The spade of archaeology has provided tens of thousands of discovered biblical sites that had been lot to the recent knowledge of man. One example would be the great city of Nineveh. The city of Nineveh has a central position in the Old Testament. But it was destroyed three-thousand years ago and was quickly forgotten but to history. Critics in our time pointed to it as proof that the Bible was just collection of fairy tells! Until, that is when an archaeologist named Claudius J. Rich discovered it in the early part of the nineteenth century! Scientific proof! Also, the Bible told us that the earth was actually round centuries before that discovery by man, "It is he that sitteth upon the circle of the earth..." Isaiah 40:22. Before that time man thought that the earth was flat! Scientific proof! There are many more examples of scientific proof that can be found by the bible student.

So now, knowing and understanding that the Bible is of divine inspiration and authority. When the Bible student studies the book, he must understand that it is THE book and not just a book. We must have a desire to know the book. We must approach our study with a bowed head and a bended knee. We must have a passion to understand God's Word. We must pray before our study for God to shine the light of discernment upon us. We must strive to be obedient; God will not teach us if we do not wish to obey His Word! Take notes! Buy a good wide-margin King James Version Bible and take notes so that years later you will have a reminder. The Bible will only improve your life!

The material for this manuscript has been influenced by dozens of books, twenty years of reading and study of the Bible, and conversations with many learned men and women. This manuscript was written for the beginner Bible student and is not exhaustive. In each hermeneutical principle I just give a few examples and have taken great efforts to keep it focused and simple.

Introduction

Hermeneutics is the science of interpretation. Therefore, Biblical Hermeneutics is the science of biblical interpretation. Most people think that all they need to do is to read the Bible and they will fully understand it. As with all literature, this is simply not true. We must know the author, understand why he is writing on this subject, and understand his style of writing to understand the work. With the Bible this is even more complicated since the Bible is a compilation of sixty-six books written by forty different authors, writing in different styles and in different time periods. Also, the Bible has within it, history, poetry, personnel letters, a book of advice, a song book, and much prophecy.

"In its technical meaning, Hermeneutics is often defined as the science and art of biblical interpretation. Hermeneutics is considered a science because it has rules, and these rules can be classified into an orderly system. It is considered an art because communication is flexible, and therefore a mechanical and rigid application of rules will sometimes distort the true meaning of a communication." "To be a good interpreter one must learn the rules of Hermeneutics as well as the art of applying those rules."

If we do not interpret the Bible correctly, we will misinterpret God's Word. Then, it will no longer be God's Word, but only our own words. Nobody cares about our words because they are not important, but God's Words are everything. Nobody likes to have his or her words taken out of context. This is especially the fact with God. People who intentionally misinterpret the Word of God are involuntary agents for the dark side. The Bible is God's Truth and Light but only if it is handled correctly and with skill. In Jesus' day the Pharisees did just that and were rebuked for being ignorant (Matthew 22:29). Let us not fall into the same trap!

Every morning I like to drink a cup of coffee and read the newspaper. I think that is how most people start off their day. Well, anyone who reads the newspaper every day will understand that a paper will always have a political slant. Some papers in the United States are conservative but most tend to be liberal. This affects how the news is interpreted and written in the paper. A reader must consider the editor of the paper, the owner, the journalist, and of what country they are from. All of this affects the outlook of the paper and the writing which goes into it. All of this must be understood by the reader, or he shall be led astray by others political viewpoint. The same could be made by books. Shakespeare was a fine author, but if you understood the man and how he wrote, you can understand his writing in a much fuller manner, and his work will come alive for you. That is called Shakespearean Hermeneutics.

God's Word is even more important. We must understand all of the principals involved to fully understand what God is telling us. The Bible student will discover that if they will follow these basic hermetical principles that the Scripture will literally interpret itself. God has written His Word so that even the simplest among us can easily read and understand for himself. Once we read and understand, then it is our responsibility to apply the knowledge to our lives for our edification. When we edify ourselves then we will edify the Church.

There may be many applications of Scripture but there is only one interpretation. That is the interpretation that God intended it to have. While reading the Bible we interpret it using the literal method unless the text implies otherwise. The literal method means to understand using everyday normal language that has the everyday straight forward meaning. If I said that there is a cow in the field eating, that is exactly what I mean. Because the inspired writers of the New Testament quoted hundreds of verses using the literal method, it could even be said that it is the approved method of the Holy Spirit. Whenever Jesus or the church leaders used the Old Testament, they always used the literal sense. There is figurative language, poetry and even a few allegories used in Scripture. But these literary tools are only used to enhance the literal use. These figures of speech must be located, and understood why they are being used, and interpret them correctly.

For example, symbols, if the verse is not clearly symbolic, no symbolism should be forced upon it. If it is clearly symbolic, the symbols must be interpreted literally. Sometimes angels are symbolized as stars. But we understand that angels are a literal entity.

Here in the United States, we live in a Jesus saturated culture that is biblical illiterate! There is a church on every street corner filled with Bibles. Most private homes have at least one Bible inside. Yet only a small minority of people have actually read the book in it's entirely. In our soap opera culture and with so little biblical knowledge there is a recipe for wild stories and false doctrines preached by spiritual snake oil salesmen in the world and even within the church.

When the children of Israel returned from captivity, they were ignorant of God's Law. They had been living in bondage in Babylon and were now speaking another language, which was Aramaic. Ezra, the priest had to read the Law to the people and give the proper interpretation. "So, they read in the book in the law of God distinctly, and gave the sense, and caused them to understand the reading" (Nehemiah 8:8). Ezra and the Priests did not just leave the reading of the law to chance; they "distinctly gave the sense" and "caused them to understand." That is what Biblical Hermeneutics can do for us today. It can give us the sense and cause us to understand God's Word.

Allegory Principle

An allegory is a story put together with several points of comparison. It is a continued metaphor and Hypo catastasis.

Allegory, a very legitimate way of teaching truth, should not be confused with allegorizing, which takes a narrative that was not meant to teach truth by identification. By a point-by-point comparison, allegorical makes the narrative convey ideas different from those intended by the original author. Thus, allegorical is an arbitrary way of handling any narrative.[1]

Few figures have been the subject of greater controversy than *Allegory*; or, have been more variously defined. One class of Rhetoricians declare that it is a continued metaphor: and another class declare that it is not. But as is often the case under such circumstances, neither is quite correct, because both have a part of the truth and put it for the whole. Neither of the contending parties takes into consideration the existence of hypo catastasis. And this fact accounts for the confusion, not only with regard to allegory, but also with regard to metaphor.

All three figures are based on comparison. Simile is comparison by resemblance; metaphor is comparison by representation; hypo catastasis is comparison by implication.

In the first comparison is stated; in the second it is substituted; the third it is implied.

Thus, Allegory is a continuation of the latter two, metaphor or hypo catastasis; while the parable (q.v.) is a continuation of the Simile.

---

[1] Mickelson, A. Berkeley. *Interpreting the Bible.* William B. Eerdmans Publishing Company, Grand Rapids, MI., p. 231. 1963.

This definition clears the whole ground, and explains the whole of the difficulties, and reconciles the different schools. The Allegory, therefore, is of two kinds; one in which it is continued metaphor (as in Psalm 23), where the two things are both mentioned (Jehovah, and the Shepherd's care) and what is asserted belongs to the principal object; the other, in which it is continued hypo catastasis (Ps. 80:8-15), where only one thing is mentioned (the vine), and what is asserted belongs properly to the second object; vis., to Israel. Israel whom it really refers, is not mentioned, but only implied.

Figure 1: The Bible

Allegory thus differs from *Parable,* for a *parable* is a *continued Simile*. It never departs from the simple statement that the one thing resembles another. While the allegory *represents*, or *implies*, that the one thing is the other. As in the allegory of the Pilgrim's Progress: What is spoken of one person refers to another person in similar circumstances and experiences. In Psalm. 80 and Is. 5., what is spoken of a Vine refers to Israel: but, in Genesis, what is stated of Israel and Ishmael, Sarah and Hagar are all true history, yet in Gal. 4 it is made to speak of and set forth other truths, and hence there it is, and is called an "Allegory" (Gal. 4:24).

The modern and common usage of the word allegory is thus quite different from the Scriptural definition. According to the modern sense it is taken to mean a fictitious narrative which has another and deeper meaning than that which is expressed.

An allegory may sometimes be fictitious, but Gal. 4 shows us that a true history may be allegorized (*i.e.*, be shown to have further teaching in that which actually took place) without detracting from the truth of the history. Here notes this important fact: that, in either case, Allegory is always stated in the *past* tense, and never in the future. Allegory is thus distinguished from Prophecy. The Allegory brings other teaching out of past events, while the prophecy tells us events that are yet to come and means exactly what is said.[2]

Principles for Interpreting Allegories

1. Be able to state explicitly who were the original hearer or readers. This will enable you to see the allegory as a living vehicle of teaching rather than a literary form in an ancient narrative.

2. If possible, note why the allegory was told in the first place. What was the point in telling it to begin with?

3. Search out the basic points of comparison stressed by the original speaker or writer. The allegory itself usually makes these clear by the emphasis put upon particular elements in the story.

4. After listing the basic points of comparison and the things for which they stand, state in as simple a manner as possible why these truths were essential for the original hearers or readers and why they are essential for us today.

Here listed is a small example of some of the allegories found in the Bible. This is not a complete list.

---

[2] Bullinger, Ethelbert William. *Figures of Speech used in the Bible.* Baker Book House, Grand Rapids, MI., ps. 748-749. 1897.

Jacob's Blessing- Genesis 49:   The prophetical blessing of Jacob can be labeled as an allegory.

The Vine of Israel- Psalm 80:8-16: Song of Solomon: The book Song of Solomon is an allegory of the love of God and His people. First Israel and now the Church.

The Bed- Isaiah 28:20: This is an *Allegory*:   The prophet is speaking of the great fear which should have stirred up the people of Judea at the speedy coming of Sennacherib; but they preferred to left in their false security.   By this beautiful allegorical illustration, they are informed that their rest should be restless, and their sleep should be soon disturbed.

> *"For the bed is shorter than that a man can stretch himself on it: and the covering narrower than that he can wrap himself in it."*

The Good Tree, Wheat and Chaff- Matthew 3:10,12: Both of these allegories are about judgment by God whose lives do not match the desires of God's Word. Jesus wanted to make this serious matter clearer to His hearers.

> *"And now also the axe is laid unto the root of the trees: therefore, every tree which bringeth not forth good fruit is hewn down, and cast into the fire."*

> *"Whose fan is in his hand, and he will throughly purge his floor, and gather his wheat into the garner; but he will burn up the chaff with unquenchable fire."*

Salt of the Earth- Matthew 5:13: A reflection of one's actions and how it is valued by God.

> *"Ye are the salt of the earth: but if the salt have lost his savour, wherewith shall it be salted? It is henceforth good for nothing, but to be cast out, and to be trodden under foot of men."*

Judging Others- Matthew 7:3-5: Here Jesus is trying to tell His hearers that Judgment is for God, who knows all, and not for other people who have no understanding.

> *"And why beholdest thou the mote that is in thy brother's eye, but considerest not the beam that is in thine own eye?"*

> *"Or how wilt thou say to thy brother, let me pull out the mote out of thine eye; and, behold, a beam is in thine own eye?"*

> *"Thou hypocrite, first cast out the beam out of thine own eye; and then shalt thou see clearly to cast out the mote out of thy brother's eye."*

Bridegroom- Matthew 9:15: Jesus here is telling us that He is the Bride of the Church that will soon come.

> *"And Jesus said unto them, can the children of the bridechamber mourn, as long as the bridegroom is with them? But the days will come, when the bridegroom shall be taken from them, and then they shall fast."*

New Cloth/Wine- Matthew 9:16-17. The "old piece" on the new implies the solemn lesson as to the impossibility of reforming the old nature. Jesus is saying that we must transform ourselves.

19

"No man putteth a piece of new cloth unto an old garment, for that which is put in to fill it up taketh from the garment, and the rent is made worse."

"Neither do men put new wine into old bottles: else the bottles break, and the wine runneth out, and the bottles perish: but they put new wine into new bottles, and both are preserved."

Figure 2: Unclean spirit

Unclean Spirit- Matthew 12:43-45: This is an *Allegory.* It is to be interpreted of the Jewish nation, as verse 45 declares. By *application* also it teaches the unclean spirit's *going out* of his own accord, and not being "cast out" (verse 28,29). When he is "cast out," he never returns; but when he "goes out," he comes back; and finds only a "reformed character," instead of the Holy Spirit indwelling in the one who is born again.

The Plough- Luke 9:62: This is a brief allegory.

"And Jesus said unto him, no man, having put his hand to the plough, and looking back, is fit for the kingdom of God."

The Harvest- John 4:35: This is a comparison of a crop and the world of lost souls.

"Say not ye, There are yet four months, and then cometh harvest? Behold, I say unto you, lift up your eyes, and look on the fields; for they are white already to harvest."

The Grafted Olive Tree- Romans 11:16-18: This is a comparison of our Christian life and an olive tree which represents Israel.

"For if the first fruit be holy, the lump is also holy: and if the root be holy, so are the branches. And if some of the branches be broken off, and thou, being a wild olive tree, wert grafted in among them, and with them partakes of the root and fatness of the olive tree;"

"Boast not against the branches. But if thou boast, thou bearest not the root, but the root thee."

Sleeping Saints- Romans 13:11-12: This is a comparison of our past and present lives.

"And that, knowing the time, that now it is high time to awake out of sleep: for now is our salvation nearer than when we believed."

"The night is far spent, the day is at hand: let us therefore cast off the works of darkness, and let us put on the armour of light."

Christian Work- 1 Corinthians 3:6-8, 12-15: This is a comparison of good and bad Christian work.

"I have planted, Apollos watered; but God gave the increase."

"So then neither is he that planteth any thing, neither he that watereth; but God that giveth the increase."

"Now he that planteth and he that watereth are one: and every man shall receive his own reward according to his own labour."

"Now if any man build upon this foundation gold, silver, precious stones, wood, hay, stubble;"

"Every man's work shall be made manifest: for the day shall declare it, because it shall be revealed by fire; and the fire shall try every man's work of what sort it is."

"If any man's work abide which he hath built thereupon, he shall receive a reward."

"If any man's work shall be burned, he shall suffer loss: but he himself shall be saved; yet so as by fire."

Leaven- 1 Corinthians 5:7-8. This is a comparison of bread and a Christian lifestyle.

"Purge out therefore the old leaven, that ye may be a new lump, as ye are unleavened. For even Christ our Passover is sacrificed for us:"

"Therefore let us keep the feast, not with old leaven, neither with the leaven of malice and wickedness; but with the unleavened bread of sincerity and truth."

Tables of Love- 2 Corinthians :2-3: This is a comparison of our earthly ministry and the Spirit.

"Ye are our epistles written in our hearts, known and read of all men: Forasmuch as ye are manifestly declared to be the epistle of Christ ministered by us, written not with ink, but with the Spirit of the living God; not in tables of stone, but in fleshly tables of the heart."

Heavenly House- 2 Corinthians 5:1: This is a comparison of our earthly home to a heavenly home.

"For we know that if our earthly house of this tabernacle were dissolved, we have a building of God, an house not made with hands, eternal in the heavens."

Spiritual Warfare- 2 Corinthians 10:3-5: This is a comparison of Roman strongholds and Spiritual battles.

"For though we walk in the flesh, we do not war after the flesh:"

"(For the weapons of our warfare are not carnal, but mighty through God to the pulling down of strongholds;)"

" Casting down imaginations, and every high thing that exalteth itself against the knowledge of God, and bringing into captivity every thought to the obedience of Christ;"

Virgin to Christ- 2 Corinthians 11:2: This is a comparison of earthly marriage and our relationship to God.

> *"For I am jealous over you with godly jealousy: for I have espoused you to one husband, that I may present you as a chaste virgin to Christ."*

Sowing to the Spirit- Galatians 6:8:

> *"For he that soweth to his flesh shall f the flesh reap corruption; but he that soweth to the Spirit shall of the Spirit reap life everlasting."*

Armor of God- Ephesians 6:10-18: This is a well-known comparison of Roman armor and Spiritual warfare.

Figure 3: Proclaiming the Gospel

Application Principle

Applying God's Truth only after the correct interpretation has been learned. If we do not learn the correct interpretation first, the application can never be applied correctly, leading directly to false doctrine. When we learn the proper interpretation of a certain text, then we can apply its truth to our lives and community. The interpretation of a text supplies us with the meaning. When we understand the meaning of a text, then we are free to apply the meaning to our lives. Here are some examples.

The True Light- Exodus 10:21-24: The Israelite's are in Egyptian bondage and God is in the process of freeing them. The proper application of the story is that the sinner is in slavery to Satan and is in spiritual darkness, but was freed by God and brought into His Light of Salvation.

This is the application. In the ninth plague God judges the Egyptian sun god called Ra. The god Ra was the most important, and powerful of all of the Egyptian gods.

The Egyptians were being judged because they did not worship the True Light, but instead worshiped a false god they had invented. The leader of the Egyptians, Pharaoh, was trying to keep God's people in bondage. The wicked world that we live in today also is trying to keep us, God's people, in spiritual bondage. God put the Egyptians in physical darkness because they did not worship the One True God. Today there is spiritual darkness because the world does not worship the One True God.

The Israelite's had light in their dwellings, but it was not a natural light, it was a supernatural light from God. This supernatural Light shined out of their homes into a dark Egyptian land. Today, our bodies is our dwelling and temple of the Holy

25

Spirit, it is not a natural light, but a supernatural light from God. This supernatural Light shines forth out of our soul through our worship, good works and daily living in this dark world.

There was total darkness over Egypt for three days (Exodus 10:22-23). Egypt, in Scripture symbolizes the world; the world would again be in spiritual darkness while Jesus was in the tomb for three days.

Figure 4: The Bible

The Salvation of Rahab-Joshua 2: Joshua had led the people across the Jordan River and was going to attack the city of Jericho. The Israelite's were in large numbers, but Jericho was the strongest fortified city in Palestine and was confident. But Rahab, a sinner, believed the messengers of God's people and was saved.

The application is as follows. Rahab was a sinner living in a condemned city that was under the curse of God. Jericho is a type of this world. Rahab was a sinner living in a lost world, just like we are sinners living in this lost world. Rahab was a prostitute and a bad character, on her own she is a condemned person. We are spiritual prostitutes and are bad characters, and we are all condemned unless Christ saves us. There was nothing about Rahab

26

to commend her to God. There is nothing in man to commend us to God (Romans 3:10).

But Rahab had something that others in Jericho did not have, and that was she had faith in God. She heard the message given to her by God's messengers and believed the word of their God. A few in this lost world will have faith. We heard the Gospel and believed God's world. Rahab's messengers said, "Our life for yours." Here is the message Jesus Christ also have given us. His life for ours! Everyone in this world is a potential Rahab, but like then, only a few will have the faith and believe. Salvation of God comes from faith in His Word.

Achan and Ai- sin in the Church- Joshua 7-8: In Chapter 6 we have the stunning victory over the city of Jericho. That was because the people were obedient to the Lord. But after the victory they were supposed to give the wealth of the city to glorify the Lord in providing the victory. Everyone did, except one, that was Achan. A major theme of the book of Joshua is that obedience brings blessing, while disobedience brings defeat. Chapters seven and eight discuss Achan's sin and the implications of that sin on the entire house of God which Israel was at this time.

This is the application for us today in the Church. Until willful sin is purged from the Church, God's blessing will be withheld, even the giving over of some saints to the devil for correction. Jesus would later tell us that it takes only a little bit of liven to affect the whole loaf. Christians would have much more power from God if we will just be obedient and refrain from sinful behaviors. Achan's sin was committed at the time of victory for Israel, but it led to a defeat soon after.

Sin usually catches Christian's while they are on the mountain top, flush with spiritual victory. If sin is quickly repented of it's not a problem, but unrepentant sin will send a Christian or an entire Church crashing down into the valley.

David and Mephibosheth- 2 Samuel 9: This is a beautiful story reflecting that God has mercy on mankind for the sake of another, which is Jesus Christ. This is a beautiful picture of salvation by Christ.

This is the application for us today. David is now king and wishes to show the kindness of God to the house of Saul because of his covenant with Jonathan, Saul's son.

Figure 5: King David

David now had the upper hand, and no one would have found any fault with him if he had rounded up the members of Saul's family and killed them all, but David's throne became a throne of mercy rather than of judgment because of another (Jonathan). We may draw a comparison here and show that through the blood of Jesus Christ the throne of God is a throne of mercy today because of Another, God's Son. But this throne will someday become a throne of judgment because of those who reject Christ.

Verse three tells us that Jonathan had a son whose name was Mephibosheth and was lame on both feet. Mephibosheth was lame because of a fall. His nurse had dropped him when fleeing with him from the enemy. He had fallen at the hands of another. Sinful man has fallen at the hands of another, who was Adam. Every son of Adam is lame on both feet. Now where was

28

Mephibosheth? He was in the house of Machir, in the land of Lodebar. That was an interesting place, and that is just where the sinner is. Machir means "sold." Mephibosheth was living in a house of bondage. We are all sold under sin in a house of bondage- a slave of sin and a slave of Satan.

The land of Lodebar means "no pasture." Where there is no pasture there is no satisfaction. No pasture means "no peace."

We read later that David sent and fetched him. Mephibosheth did not go, he was not seeking David, and he did not fetch himself, but David sent and fetched him. When we are sinners, God sends and fetched us.

When Mephibosheth came to David, he fell on his face. He feared David. This is a picture of the sinner in fear on that great judgment day. But Mephibosheth was to be shown kindness for the sake of another. God, for Christ's sake, will save the sinner. God did not save you for your own sake, but because of another. Mephibosheth went to live in Jerusalem, which means "Peace." He came from Lodebar (no pasture) to Jerusalem, the "city of peace." Here is an opportunity to tell the sinner to leave Lodebar and move down to Jerusalem. God is already to fetch him out of Lodebar and over to Jerusalem.

The end of the story is- "so Mephibosheth did eat continually at the king's table; and was lame on both feet." The fact of the matter is, that when Mephibosheth came from Lodebar to Jerusalem, he brought his lame feet right along with him. When we came to the King's house and ate at the King's table, and became members of the family of God we brought our lame feet with us.[3]

---

[3] Hartill, J. Edwin. *Principles of Biblical Hermeneutics.* Zondervan Publishing House, Grand Rapids, MI., ps. 44-45. 1947.

Naaman and Elisha- 2 Kings 5: This has to do with a Syrian captain and the Jewish captive. Here was a little girl who believed that the prophet could heal Naaman of his leprosy.

Here is the application. Someone has said that there are millions of lepers in the world. We are not certain as to the exact number, but we do know that there are many times that number of spiritual lepers. Spiritually, every man is a leper until cleansed in the Blood. His story gives the Gospel plan of salvation.

Figure 6: Leprosy

Leprosy is a symbol of sin. Men are lepers in the sight of God, when in sin. In the nation of Israel, lepers were excluded from worship in the Temple of God, by the command of Jehovah. This was not true in any of the other nations, for lepers were allowed to mingle with the rest of the people. Sin, like leprosy, breaks out in the most loathsome forms. You can see it on all sides. Sin, like leprosy, makes everyone hideous. Sin, like leprosy, brings separation. In the nation of Israel, the leper could not come into the camp with the others. When anyone came near, he must shout, "unclean, unclean!" If the moral lepers of today had to shout, "unclean" there would be a terrific racket. Sin, like leprosy, cannot be cured by man. A sinner is a death-doomed man, and no one can cure him but God. It seems that no one could cure leprosy but God, in the Scriptures. We mentioned here that there are some ways in which the sinner and a leper are not alike. A leper never makes light of his leprosy, but a sinner does make light of his sin. The leper knows he is a leper, but the sinner fails to recognize that he is a sinner.

When a sinner is awakened to his sin, he will be miserable, as was Naaman. With all of his good things, Naaman was not happy.

The Gospel of cleansing came to Naaman through a little girl, not a great woman; but she had a great message. She had a humble position. Though she was a servant of Naaman and his wife, she was also a servant of Jehovah. Here is a lesson. The thing necessary to get Naaman into touch with God was the testimony of a servant. When this little girl started to testify, things started to move, and the king moved, and then Naaman moved over into Israel.

The law of Assyria did not bar Naaman from society, but in Israel God's law said a leper must be separated. When Naaman came into Israel, then Elisha treated him as a leper should be treated. The trouble today is that the world is trying to make sin respectful, and God will not have it so. You should treat the sinner as a sinner and put him in his place. You can never save a man by patting him on the back and then feeding him cream puffs. When the sinner takes a sinner's place, then he will be saved. There is too much fellowship with sin, and compromise with sin. Naaman had to take the leper's place before he was cleansed. The sinner must take the place of the sinner.

Naaman was willing to go far and do much, but he wanted to do things his own way. The sinner is much like Naaman, for he is not satisfied with the remedy prescribed. He will say it is too easy. A sinner never does like God's plan, and the reason is- God's plan strips the sinner of all his righteousness. It brings all sinners on the same plane.

Naaman dipped seven times. Seven is the number of God. Six is the number of evil and of man. There is no cleansing for man until six is submerged in God's seven. In Adam we are marked with six, but in Christ we are marked with seven.[4]

The Lost Sheep- Luke 15:1-7: Jesus has an audience of sinners and Pharisees and Scribes together. Because we have two different groups of people, we therefore have two different applications. A man has a hundred sheep, but one has strayed off from the ninety-nine. Jesus asked what man would not leave the ninety-nine to go and get the one that has strayed. The answer is that they all would. Jesus is saying to them that God will also.

The application to the sinners in the audience is that God loves them and will diligently seek them out and lead them home. Every sinner is precious in the sight of God, and He will call all of them home. Sheep are silly little animals. Sheep are a prey animal so they will seek the safety in the pack. But they are absent minded and will get distracted and accidentally wander off from the rest and get themselves into trouble. People are like silly sheep sometimes; we will get distracted with the cares of this world and wander off from the Kingdom. But when we come to our senses, we will also have a good shepherd by the name of Jesus Christ who will be there when we call out for help.

The application for the Scribes and Pharisees (and preachers of today) is that instead of concerning themselves with making money and keeping power to themselves they should be a shepherd to the people and be looking for the strays and bring them back home.

---

[4] Ibid, 45-46.

The Prodigal Son- Luke 15:11-32: Jesus was eating at the house of one of the chief Pharisees with other Pharisees and Scribes, on the Sabbath day (Luke 14:1). Chapter fourteen is the context setting up chapter fifteen which deals with the Prodigal Son. While Jesus is there the Pharisees bring in a sick man to see if Jesus would heal him on the Sabbath day. They are setting up Jesus so that they can accuse Him of working (healing) on the Sabbath day and kill Him. These men are considering an evil act to stop the preaching of Jesus. They know that Jesus can heal at will, they do not dispute this. Because of this they know that Jesus is from God Instead, these preachers are only concerned about their Temple money that they pocket and their positions that allow them to profit off the people. Jesus heals the sick man in their sight (Luke 14:4) and then teaches on humility, the parable of the great feast, worthless salt, the lost sheep and the lost coin. Now, Jesus sets Himself up to speak on the Prodigal Son.

This is the application. Jesus was trying to teach the Pharisees that God's will is to be humble, and love the people. They were only concerned with rules and regulations of their religious system that they had built up, not to serve God, but to serve themselves. Their concern should have been to love one another and preach in the spirit of Godly love and not out of judgment and control.

If any application is to be made to this present dispensation it must be made to people who are in a covenant relationship with God. In other words, the prodigal son is not a lost sinner but a saved sinner. He is a son. The lost sheep, the lost coin, and the lost boy all apply to the backslider. The one-hundred sheep were saved; the coins were saved; the two boys were saved. It was a sheep that was lost, not a goat. It was a real coin that was lost, not a counterfeit. It was just as good as the rest of the coins on the string. The boy was lost was just as much a son as the one who stayed at home. This boy was a son, and nothing could unmake him a son. He was a son in the home and a son when he left home, and a son when in the field feeding swine. If he had died in the far

33

country, he would have still been a son. This boy was a son even when he brought shame to the family. The parable teaches the everlasting love of God for His own. The son could waste and spend all that he had, save his father's love, but he could not spend that; and when he returned home his father met him with outstretched arms.[5]

Figure 7: Compass

_____

[5] Ibid, p. 46.

Christ- Centered Principle

In this principal Jesus Christ is shown to be written about and is the center of the entire Bible. We read of Him in the Gospels, but He is written of throughout the Old Testament and the New Testament. This is a very important principle to keep in mind while reading the Old Testament because Jesus Christ can be found throughout the Bible.

In the Gospels, Jesus Christ proclaimed this truth about Himself:

"*...in the volume of the book it is written of me...*" (Hebrew 10:7). This is reference to the Old Testament, the first five books of the Bible. Jesus Christ had arrived to replace the sacrifices of the Law and be our sacrifice for sin. Jesus Christ can be found throughout the Law of Moses.

"*Search the Scriptures...they are written which testify of me.*" (John 5:39). Here Jesus Christ himself tells us to study the Old Testament and look for Him. The Old Testament testifies of the coming of Jesus Christ, His ministry, His sacrifice and death on the Cross.

"*...believe all that the prophets have spoken: Ought not Christ to have suffered these things, and to enter into his glory? And beginning at Moses and all the prophets, he expounded unto them in all the scriptures the things concerning himself.*" (Luke 24: 25-27).

"*...all things must be fulfilled which were written in the law of Moses, and in the prophets, and in the psalms, concerning me.*" (Luke 24:44).

35

The apostles also said that this is true:

> *"To Him give all the prophets witness, that through his name whosoever believeth in him shall receive remission of sins."* (Acts 10:43).

Figure 8: Prophets

They admit that all of the prophets witnessed about Jesus Christ. Not some of the prophets, but all of them! This would include the entire Old Testament!

> *"...we have found Him of whom Moses in the law, and the prophets, did write, Jesus of Nazareth, the son of Joseph."* (John 1:45).

Here the Apostles tell us that Jesus Christ is spoken of throughout the Old Testament. The Law is a reference of the first five books of the Old Testament and the Prophets is a reference to the rest of the Old Testament.

"For by him were all things created...And he is before all things, and by him all things consist. ...that in all things He might have the preeminence." (Colossians 1:16-18).

Here the Apostle Paul admits that Jesus Christ has created all things, including Scripture and He is preeminent in Scripture.

The Apostle Paul wrote that Jesus Christ considered Himself equal with God. Being equal with God really means that He was God in the flesh.

"Who, being in the form of God, thought it not robbery to be equal with God." Philippians 2:6.

The writer of the book of Hebrews wrote that Jesus Christ is the power and authority of God, which is what this phrase means.

"...sat down on the right hand of God." Hebrews 1:3.

The writer again says the same thing but in another way.

"But unto the Son he saith, Thy throne, O God..." Hebrews 1:8.

Jesus Christ, and the Apostles said that He has created all things!

Jesus Christ had made it very clear to the Romans and the Pharisee's that He was God who had created the world. If Jesus Christ is the creator of the world, then He is the creator of the Word of God as well. That would make the Bible Christ centered!

"Jesus said unto them, Verily, verily, I say unto you, Before Abraham was, I AM!" (emphasis is mine) John 8:58.

The Apostle John repeated this in his Gospel of John.

"All things were made by him; and without him was not any thing made that was made." John 1:3.

And again, the Apostle John repeats this thought.

> *"He was in the world, and the world was made by him, and the world knew him not."* John 1:10.

Not to be out done, the Apostle Paul said the same thing in his writings to the Colossians!

> *"For by him were all things created, that are in heaven, and that are in earth, visible and invisible, whether they be thrones, or dominion, or principalities, or powers: all things were created by him, and for him: And he is before all things, and by him all things consist."* Colossians 1:16-17.

Also, later in this same book:

> *"For of him, and through him, are all things: to whom be glory for ever. Amen."* Colossians 11: 36.

Salvation of man is by Jesus Christ alone:

If this is correct then Jesus Christ is indeed the center theme of the entire Bible since the Bible's story is centered on the salvation of sinful man! The Apostle Peter gives us the Plan of Salvation.

> *"Then Peter said unto them, Repent, and be baptized every one of you in the name of Jesus Christ for the remission of sins, and ye shall receive the gift of the Holy Ghost."* Acts 2:38.

And again, Peter repeats this before the Council of the Sanhedrin.

> *"Neither is there salvation in any other: for there is none other name under heaven given among men, whereby we must be saved."* Acts 4:12.

John the Baptist also proclaimed the salvation of man of his sins by Jesus Christ as told by the Apostle John in his Gospel.

"The next day John seeth Jesus coming unto him, and saith, Behold the Lamb of God, which taketh away the sins of the world." John 1:29.

As we can see from the Bible itself and the testimony of Jesus Christ and some of the Apostles is that Christ is spoken of throughout the Scriptures and is the central theme of the Bible.

Figure 9: The Bible

Compound Names of God Principle

By understanding the compound names of God in the Old Testament we can gain a better understanding of the nature of God and what He is to us. This is a small minor principle, but can be useful while reading Scripture and how it can apply to our individual lives. The Lord's names are an insight into His personality.

1. **Jehovah-Jireh:** This name means that "The Lord will provide." It can be found in Genesis 22:14, where Abraham names the place where he built an alter to sacrifice his son, Isaac. The Lord provided a ram for sacrifice instead. It was fulfilled by Jesus Christ, on the Cross whereby His sacrifice sin was dealt with, as we read in Hebrews 10:10-12.

2. **Jehovah-Rapha:** This name means "The Lord that heals." It can be found in Exodus 15:26. This is the first mention of the blessings of obedience found in Deut. 7:12-15 and 28. It was fulfilled by Jesus Christ before the Cross, as told in 1 Peter 2:24, *"...by whose stripes ye were healed."*

3. **Jehovah-Nissi:** This name means "The Lord our banner or victory." It can be found in Exodus 17:15. It was fulfilled by Jesus Christ in 1 Corinthians 15:57, *"But thanks be to God, which giveth us the victory through our Lord Jesus Christ."*

4. **Jehovah-M'Kaddesh:** This name means "The Lord that sanctifies." It can be found in Exodus 31:13. It was fulfilled by Jesus Christ at the Cross as seen in Hebrews 10:10, *"By the which will we are sanctified through the offering of the body of Jesus Christ once for all."*

5. **Jehovah-Shalom:** This name means "The Lord our peace." It can be found in Judges 6:24. It was fulfilled by Jesus Christ in John 16:33, *"These things I have spoken unto you, that in me ye might have peace..."*

6. **Jehovah-Saboath:** This name means "The Lord of Hosts or warfare, or Almighty." It can be found in 1 Samuel 1:3. It was fulfilled by Jesus Christ in James 5:4-7, *"...are entered into the ears of the Lord of sabaoth..."*

7. **Jehovah-Elyon:** This name means "The Lord most high." It can be found in Psalm 7:17. It was fulfilled in Luke 1:32, 76, 78 *"He shall be great, and shall be called the Son of the Highest..."*

8. **Jehovah-Raah:** This name means "The Lord my shepherd." It can be found in Psalm 23:1. It was fulfilled in Jesus Christ, whom is our Chief Shepherd as seen in 1 Peter 5:4; John 10:11. *"And when the chief Shepherd shall appear..." "I am the good shepherd..."*

9. **Jehovah-Hoseenu:** This name means "The Lord our maker." It can be found in Psalm 95:6. It was fulfilled at creation as revealed to John the Apostle in John 1:3. *"All things were made by him; and without him was not anything made that was made."*

10. **Jehovah-Tsidkenu:** This name means "The Lord our righteousness." It can be found in Jeremiah 23:6. It was fulfilled by Jesus Christ as revealed in 1 Corinthians 1:30. *"But of him are ye in Christ Jesus, who of God is made unto us wisdom, and righteousness, and sanctification, and redemption."*

11. **Jehovah-Shammah:** This name means "The Lord is present." It can be found in Ezekiel 48:35. It is fulfilled in Jesus Christ by His own testimony in Matthew 28:20. *"Teaching them to observe all things whatsoever I have*

commanded you: and, lo, I am with you always, even unto the end of the world. Amen."

Figure 10: The Bible

Context Principle

The Context Principle is where the Bible student keeps Scripture in the same context in which it was intended by the author, and to keep it's same meaning intact.

The most common source of false doctrine and Christian cultist beliefs is the misinterpretation of Scripture, knowingly or through ignorance, by taking it out of its intended context. Knowing the context is the key to knowing the mind of God through His Word. Every verse must be studied in the context that God has given it. We should never take a verse out of its setting and give it a different meaning. By taking Scripture out of its context we only deceive ourselves.

Nobody makes isolated statements. Everything we say and think is in a certain context Without context nothing would make since! The Word of God is no exception. God had His Word written in His context. By not knowing the context of Scripture we will most certainly misinterpret God's Word. Here are five easy rules for finding the context.

1. Carefully observe the immediate context; that which precedes and follows the passage. This usually tells you the most about your target passage. This is called the "near" or "immediate" context. If the key to the context is several chapters before your target passage, this is called the "remote" context.

2. Carefully observe any parallel thoughts in the same book to the materials in the passage being interpreted. Be aware of the purposes and development of thought in the book. I call this the "contextual flow." The contextual flow is especially important in the Gospels and the New Testament. It seems these texts were well thought out before the writing and written in one setting. We should also read these books in one setting.

3. Carefully observe any parallel thought in another book by the same author or in other books by different authors. Consider the purpose and development of thought in these books.

4. Have a good understanding of metaphors, shadows and types, and other figures of speech. The Bible is full of these figures of speech! We must recognize them and understand what they are telling us. If we fail at this then all kinds of silly doctrines could be imagined!

5. Bear in mind that the smaller the quantity of material to be interpreted, the greater the danger of ignoring the context. No axiom is better known and more frequently disobeyed than the oft quoted: "A text without a context is only a pretext." Somehow, to discern this kind of error in someone else is easy but to recognize this same fault in us is most difficult.[6]

Here are some of the most misinterpreted verses of the Bible. Let us go through them and find the correct interpretation, using the correct context.

Baptism for the dead- 1 Corinthians 15: The Mormon Church (LDS) believes that a living church member, in good standing, can go to their Temple and baptize themselves in the place for people long dead, and baptize and provide salvation in their stead. They use 1 Corinthians 15:29 as their justification for their strange doctrine. "Else what shall they do which are baptized for the dead, if the dead rise not at all? Why are they then baptized for the dead?" They have taken this one verse and built an entire doctrine from it.

If we read the entire book at once, we can fully understand the context and the contextual flow of the book. The "dead" in chapter fifteen is a reference to Christ. This is reveled in verse

_____

[6] Mickelson, A. Berkeley. *Interpreting the Bible.* William B. Eerdmans, Grand Rapids, MI., p. 113. 1963.

twelve of the same chapter. "Now if Christ be preached that he rose from the dead, how say some among you that there is no resurrection of the dead?" Now knowing this, to better understand verse twenty-nine substitute "Christ" for "dead." Chapter fifteen starts with the explanation of the resurrection of Christ, and then uses that example to explain our own resurrection. This is a beautiful chapter of the Word of God, and it is the full mention of our own resurrection. It is a shame that it has been sullied by misinterpretation!

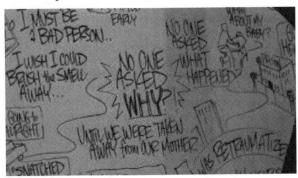

Figure 11: Context

Paul's choice of the word "they" in verse twenty-nine is not a reference to a group of people or Christians as the Mormons claim, but just an indirect reference to the fact that Paul baptized very few persons himself. This fact Paul states himself in chapter one verse fourteen through seventeen. In twenty-five years of ministry Paul baptized only two persons and one household himself. Paul did not feel called to baptize but to preach the Gospel. The Apostle Paul always allowed the local church leaders do all of the baptizing.

Faith- Psalm 23: Most people consider this beautiful Psalm to be about a thanksgiving on God's blessing. It really is not about thanksgiving, but it is about faith. In order to see this, we must read Psalm twenty-two; this is the psalm that sets up psalm twenty-three. "My God, my God, why hast thou forsaken me?"

Also, "O my God, I cry in the daytime, but thou hearest not." Psalm twenty-two is a cry for help when God seems distant. It is a cry for help when you cannot find God or His Presence.

Now read psalm twenty-three. David' reaction to the absence of God 'Presence is an explosion of faith! "The LORD is my shepherd; I shall not want." And again, "He restoreth my soul." We should always read these two psalms together because twenty-two sets up the meaning and beauty of twenty-three!

Valley of the dry bones- Ezekiel 37: This is not the Church as some will say. The eleventh verse clearly states that this is a vision of "the whole house of Israel." Chapter thirty-six speaks on God blessing Israel once more. Starting at verse sixteen of chapter thirty-six speaks of Israel's new life. Then we now have the vision of the dry bones.

Starting at verse fifteen the prophecy begins to speak of the future unity of Judah and Israel. The vision of the dry bones is a vision of this future unity and restoration in the Promised Land. Looking at the proceeding chapter and then the whole of chapter thirty-seven we can see the flow of the context that God has given it. It clearly does not speak of the Church.

Let's look at the context of the times. The prophet Ezekiel was in exile in Babylon like the rest of the people of Israel. The people were wondering and even fearful that they would never see the Promised Land again. They needed and wanted hope. God sent this series of prophecies through Ezekiel in order to tell the people that the House of Israel would be restored in due time. And it was restored exactly as the LORD had said!

Robbing God- Malachi 3:7-11: "Will a man rob God?" This is the most widely used verse today and is used in conjunction with tithing or church giving. It is many a preacher's sugar stick. But, sadly, it is used out of its context on purpose.

Let's put the book in its proper context. The priests had got accustomed to spending large amounts of money on themselves instead of the Kingdom of God as the Temple tithing system was designed to do. The priest's in the countryside were withholding the full amount of the tithes from the temple. When the money reached the temple, it was skimmed off by the temple priests. Due to this corruption the Kingdom of God and the temple services were being neglected.

CONTEXT

Figure 12: Context

In the first chapter of the book of Malachi God tells the Jewish people how much He loves them and that they are still His people. Then (1:6) God rebukes the priests for being corrupt. Starting at the tenth verse of chapter two God then rebukes the people for abandoning the Law of Moses. In (2:17) God warns of the coming judgment for their sins. In (3:6) God then commands the priests and Levites to stop robbing God by stealing the tithes. In (3:13) God then promises mercy if the Israelite would obey from then on. Chapter four is about the coming of the Messiah, which indeed happened about four-hundred years later with the birth of Jesus Christ.

The book of Malachi is all about the priests of that day and the sins in which they were involved. The priests were irreverent and neglectful. The priests were offering worthless animals (1:8) in sacrifice to God that they would not offer to the governor. They refused to work except for money (1:10). Mixed marriages became common (2:11), some would even divorce their Jewish wives to make this possible (2:14).

Fool's- Matthew 5:22: Jesus says that one who calls a brother a fool is in danger of hellfire, yet He calls the Pharisees fools in 23:17-19. Some have said that Jesus is contradicting Himself, let's look at it.

In the first instance that Matthew brings this up is when Jesus is in Galilee on a mountain. The great crowds followed Him, but the disciples followed Jesus to the top of the mountain. Those that were willing to climb the mountain were the ones who received the insightful teaching. There Jesus gave the famous Beatitudes sermon. Part of this sermon was about anger, and what it can lead into. Talking about anger is the context for calling someone a "fool" in this instant.

The Greek word here is "Moros," which has a meaning of "moral stupidity." God has given everyone a basic understanding of right and wrong and we have all been given a moral compass to follow. Plus, we all have Scripture available to us and God's Spirit is always available to those open to Him.

For a man to call another man "morally stupid," is evil and not true. Jesus did not have to tell His disciple this for they already understood that all know right and wrong from birth.

Matthew relates in the second instance that Jesus is speaking to the Pharisees in the temple, Jesus was there teaching and then tells the Scribes and Pharisees that they are a bunch of "blind fools" and that they are stealing and robbing God and the people in general.

Matthew is trying to tell them that being a spiritual leader, leading people astray spiritually, and stealing the churches money for your own benefit will put you in danger of hellfire. God is not contradicting Himself, but instead is trying to teach us a valuable lesson. If you want to be a priest or a preacher, you have to be honest with your position and the money in your charge. If not, it does not matter who you are, or what you have done, you are in danger of hellfire in eternity!

Persecutions- Matthew 10:34: "Think not that I am come to send peace on the earth: I come not to send peace, but a sword." What! This sounds like the Prince of Peace wants to start a war. If we take this verse out of its proper context it could seem to mean that Jesus wants us to wage war. Now then, you may think that is silly, but we can clearly see that some people do not need much to fall into false doctrine. That is why we never take a verse out of its context.

At the beginning of chapter ten, Jesus is about to send out the twelve disciples out into the land to preach the Word of God. They will go out alone and will experience persecution (10:14). Starting at verse sixteen Jesus warns them about persecution and how to deal with it. Jesus understands that many people will resent their message and be filled with hate and rage and persecute them.

When Jesus speaks of a sword in verse thirty-four, He is speaking of the Word of God not an actual metallic sword. The Word of God will divide the people into those who believe, and those who do not. The sword has always symbolized the Word of God in the Bible. Spouses will be divided. Father and son will be divided. Siblings will be divided. Jesus is getting His disciples ready for this type of conflict. By reading the flow of Scripture before and after the target verse, we can clearly see the proper context.

Purgatory- Matthew 12:32; 1 Corinthians 3:11-15: Purgatory is a widespread doctrine of the Catholic Church, among others. They formed this false doctrine by taking two separate

51

verses, from two separate books of the Bible, by two different authors out of their proper context, and making them mean something altogether different. Let us take a look at it.

Matthew wrote in his Gospel, "And whosoever speaketh a word against the Son of man, it shall be forgiven him: but whosoever speaketh against the Holy Ghost, it shall not be forgiven him, neither in this world, neither in the world to come." Matthew 12:32.

The last part of this verse is what is of interest, "neither in the world to come." This is just a vague reference to eternity, heaven or hell. There is no mention of which "world" is coming, nor should there be any, since the context is speaking of something else entirely, which is blasphemy. Let me explain further.

Figure 13: Purgatory?

Jesus went into the synagogue and healed some people on the Sabbath day. The local Pharisee called Jesus out for that saying that Jesus was using demonic powers in order to heal. The truth was the Pharisee could not heal anyone nor tell them how to get healed and then arrives Jesus, who heals everyone present. The local Pharisee felt very small and insecure. Their prideful spirits were crushed!

Jesus uses this opportunity to teach a lesson about maliciously misrepresenting the work of the Holy Spirit. To know of, and to be, or was, filled with the Holy Spirit and then to say it is all the work of the devil is an unforgivable sin. This is the context of this half of chapter twelve. The idea of purgatory is nowhere to be found.

The second verse that people take out of context to mean purgatory is found in 1 Corinthians 3:11-15. Let us start with verse fourteen, "If any man's work abide which he hath built thereupon, he shall receive a reward. If any man's work shall be burned, he shall suffer loss: but he himself shall be saved; yet so as by fire."

It is the last part of verse fifteen here that is of interest, "...but he himself shall be saved; yet so as by fire." There is no mention of any place called purgatory here. In chapter three of this book, Paul is speaking of being a servant of God in His Kingdom. When Christ's Blood saves us, we then work in His Kingdom doing good works, building up the Kingdom. If our works are good and holy and from God, then they will be cast into the fire of judgment and will be proven to be righteous. That saint will receive a reward in accordance with his work and the natural talents he had in this world. If our works are not from God, but are selfish, they will be thrown into the fire of judgment and will be burned up like chaff. The saint will be saved, but he shall receive no reward in heaven.

The reward of a Christian is to enter Heaven for eternity and to see the face of Jesus Christ, and to partake of God's Righteousness. Revelation 22:4. 1 John 3:2. Matthew 5:8-12, 25:21-23.

So, we have reviewed both of these verses and have found out that both have been taken out of their proper context and used for something entirely different. We must keep all Scripture in its context!

Transfiguration- Matthew 17:1-13: Some folks have said that verse Matthew 16:28 proves that Jesus would make His second return during the lifetime of the disciples. You can only believe this by taking this verse out of its context. Let us take a look at it.

Six days before the transfiguration Jesus and His disciples were along the coast of Caesarea Philippi. Jesus asks Peter who he thought that He was. Peter said that he thought Jesus was the "Christ." Later, Jesus mentions that "There be some standing here, which shall not taste of death, till they see the Son of man coming in His Kingdom (Matthew 16:28)."

Well, only six days later Jesus took Peter, James, and John up on a high mountain, it was probably Mt. Herman, "And was transfigured before them: and His face did shine as the sun, and His raiment was white as the light (Matthew 17:2)." This is what Jesus referred to as "coming in His Kingdom." The context of chapter sixteen blends right in with chapter seventeen. To not understand this, verse twenty-eight of chapter sixteen will be misinterpreted.

The Lords Supper- Matthew 26:26-29: Roman Catholics around the world take communion and actually believe that Christ's flesh and blood is in the wafer and wine at the communion table. This is not true at all, this is taking a metaphor and making it literal. Jesus was just giving the disciples a simple metaphor of the two different sacrifices in each covenant (Moses' Covenant and the New Covenant). There are many metaphors in the Bible; we must know them, understand them, before we interpret Scripture. Jesus also said He was the "door," is He really a "door," of course not, it is just a metaphor to teach us. Well, the bread and wine symbolizing the body and blood of Christ is the same, just a metaphor.

God provided the blood for the Old Testament alter in Exodus 24:8, now He does again through Jesus in Matthew 26:28. Sins can only be remitted by blood (Hebrews 9:22). Jesus was just referring to

His upcoming death, sacrifice, and resurrection to fulfill our salvation.

Thirty Silver Coins- Matthew 27:9-10: Jesus in referring to a prophecy of the prophet Zechariah 11:12, proclaimed it to be from the prophet Jeremiah. Some folks have said that this is a mistake This was not a mistake, but quite intentional. It was the custom of that day to refer to all of the prophets by just one of the Major Prophets, in this case, Jeremiah. This is never done today but was common in Jesus' day. That is the historical context.

Rewards- 1 Corinthians 3:6-15: Some people have said that there are no rewards in heaven. They have said that heaven itself is the reward. Well, heaven will surely be rewarding, and it is our eternal reward. But there are additional rewards that will be given to those who have built up God's Kingdom and have used their talents in this life doing God's work.

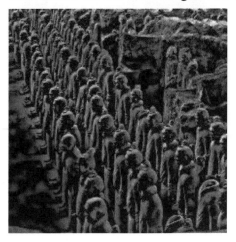

Figure 14: The Judgement

Let us now look at the context of what I am talking about. In the first chapter of First Corinthians the apostle Paul writes about the power and wisdom of Christ. In chapter two he writes about the message of the crucified Christ, then on God's wisdom. After this is established, Paul then writes about how to be a servant of God.

We are servants of God when we witness, teach, and preach to others about Christ (3:6-7). Each one building upon the others works with the help of God (3:7). In the end God will give us a reward according to our labors (3:8). Together, we are building God's building (3:9). The foundation of this building is Jesus Christ, and everyone we bring to salvation is then a part of that building (3:11). This work will be judged by fire, good work in building God's building will be proved good, unworthy work will be consumed by the fire (3:13-15).

Working out salvation- Philippians 2:12: "…work out your own salvation with fear and trembling." Many silly things have been said and written about this last half of verse twelve. It is a great verse of Christian humility and liberty in Christ. The contextual flow begins at the first chapter where the apostle Paul writes that to live is Christ. Chapter two then explains Christ's humility and greatness, commonly referred as "the kenosis. The Apostle Paul speaks on the humility of Christ's life, and it was that humility before God and man (2:7) that made Him great in the Kingdom of God (2:9).

Now then, that is the context upon which we find verse twelve. We work out our salvation through "fear and trembling," because of the humility that Jesus showed the world, we should emulate that humility ourselves. We should always be fearful to show pride in our lives. The meaning of this verse is revealed by the context of the first two chapters.

Clearly this was written so that Christians will emulate this same example. So then, in that light we need to "work out our own salvation. But how do we "work it out?" Well, the next two verses tell us, "For it is God which worketh in you both to will and to do of His good pleasure. Do all things without murmurings and disputing" (2:13-14).

Covenant Principle

This is an oral or written agreement between mankind and God. Some are conditional, in which they depend upon man's fulfillment of it. Some are Unconditional, in which it only depends on God's fulfillment on it. Four have signs from God, but three do not. There are seven total covenants.

In today's terms a covenant is a contract. A legal agreement between God and man. They have been drawn up by God, in His Grace, with different people, at different periods, and for different purposes. It is important for the Bible student to learn of these contracts, their provisions, parties involved, and their purpose.

Eden's Covenant: This covenant is found in Genesis 1:28-30 and 2:15-17. This covenant orders life in the Garden of Eden and Adam's relationship with God. This covenant is conditional; it depends on Adam being obedient. This covenant was current from the creation of Adam to the expulsion from Eden. It is no longer in force today.

"And God blessed them, and God said unto them, be fruitful and multiply, and replenish the earth, and subdue it: and have dominion over the fish of the sea, and over the fowl of the air, and over every living thing that moveth upon the earth."

"And God said, Behold, I have given you every herb bearing seed, which is upon the face of all the earth, and every tree, in the which is the fruit of a tree yielding seed; to you it shall be for meat."

"And to every beast of the earth, and to every fowl of the air, and to everything that creepeth upon the earth, wherein there is life, I have given every green herb for meat: and it was so."

"And the Lord God took the man, and put him into the Garden of Eden to dress it and to keep it."

And the Lord God commanded the man, saying, of every tree of the garden thou mayest freely eat:

But of the tree of the knowledge of good and evil, thou shalt not eat of it: for in the day that thou eatest thereof thou shalt surely die."

Here are the contents and requirements of Eden's covenant:

1.   Produce a lot of children (Genesis 1:28). God's first command to Mankind was to have a lot of children. A command we today routinely ignore. To "multiply" means to have a great number. God did not say to not have children or even to add. God commanded us to multiply! Instead today we take a little man-made pill to close the womb that God have opened for us. This is rebellion against God's Word and His Will! Today we would rather spend our money on luxury items, and vacations, on ourselves than to spend it on a large family as God commanded us.

2.   Subdue the earth (Genesis 1:28). God commanded us to subdue the earth and all of its life forms for the benefit of mankind. Man was created spiritually superior to all other life on the earth and therefore it is ours to subdue.

3.   Have dominion over the earth (Genesis 1:28). We were created in God's own image (Genesis 1:27), not any of the animals or even the earth itself. Therefore, it is for us to have dominion over the earth and its creatures.

4. They are to be vegetarians (Genesis 1:29). God gave mankind all of the fruit from the trees and plants of the earth to eat. God did not give animals to eat at this time, but He will add animals to our diet in Noah's covenant. This also went for the animals as well (Genesis 1:30). Animals could only eat fruit and plants, not other animals or man.

5. Adam must dress the garden (Genesis 2:15). Adam was commanded to dress the garden and to make it looking nice and to keep it functional. Even thou it was the Garden of Eden, I'm sure the trees still needed to be trimmed and so forth. Men were designed to work, and Adam was no exception.

6. Adam must keep the garden (Genesis 2: 15). It seems that Adam was also to keep the garden safe and in his possession. To keep it physically or spiritually, or from whom, we really do not know.

7. Adam must not eat of the tree of good and evil (Genesis 2: 17). The first six contents of the covenant were for Adam to do. The last thing God mentioned was one thing he could not do. I am very sure this last item got Adams attention more than the others. Especially since God in His good humor, put this "forbidden tree" smack in the middle of the garden! I'm very certain the fruit of this tree probably looked very delicious! The first six things Adam did very well, but unfortunately, he also eventually did the last one too. God had said if he did eat of the tree of good and evil, he would certainly die. This was true. Adam died physically and also spiritually. The Apostle Paul would later write, "For the wages of sin is death; but the gift of God is eternal life through Jesus Christ our Lord" (Romans 6:23). Adam rejected this gift and chose death instead!

Eden's covenant began with Adam and Eve in the Garden of Eden enjoying eternal life with God. The covenant ended with sin introduced into the world which brought physical and spiritual death.

Adam's Covenant: This covenant is found in Genesis 3: 14-19. This is an unconditional covenant, which means the God will fulfill all of the requirements. It consists of many curses for disobedience but one great promise of redemption. This covenant is current from the expulsion from Eden until the end of the current world. So, it is still in force today.

> *"And the Lord God said unto the serpent, because thou hast done this, thou art cursed above all cattle, and above every beast of the field; upon thy belly shalt thou go, and dust shalt thou eat all the days of thy life:"*

> *"And I will put enmity between thee and the woman, and between thy seed and her seed; it shall bruise thy head, and thou shalt bruise his heel."*

> *"Unto the woman he said, Because thou hast hearkened unto the voice of thy wife, and hast eaten of the tree, of which I commanded thee, saying, Thou shalt not eat from it: cursed is the ground for thy sake; in sorrow shalt thou eat of it all the days of thy life; Thorns also and thistles shall it bring forth to thee; and thou shalt eat the herb of the field;"*

> *"In the sweat of thy face shalt thou eat bread, till thou return unto the ground; for out of it wast thou taken: for dust thou art, and unto dust shalt thou return."*

Adam 's covenant consists of fourteen curses and a great promise for the future.

1. The serpent is cursed above all creatures (Genesis 3:14). This is still true even today. Most human beings are afraid of snakes, or any reptile for that matter, instinctively. The only exceptions are people who are raised with snakes at childhood, like the snake people of India. Even harmless grass snakes that only eat insects and don't even have teeth put ear into the average person.

2. The serpent must crawl on its belly (Genesis 3:14). From the textual context here, it is implied that serpents had legs. Snakes probably had four legs like other reptiles.

3. The serpent shall eat dust (Genesis 3:14). Snakes today spend their entire lives crawling around in the dirt. They are bound to eat a lot of dust if only by accident.

4. The serpent and women shall be enemies (Genesis 3:15). Almost all women around the world are afraid of snakes and most or all reptiles. This is pretty much a universal trait for women. This is an instinct that God has placed on the hearts of women.

5. The serpents and woman's descendants will be enemies (Genesis 3:15). Eve was never afraid of serpents before, that is why she so freely spoke to one. All of her descendants are now naturally afraid of serpents. This fear goes all the way back to the Garden of Eden.

6. The serpent shall be crushed by the woman's seed (Genesis 3:15). This is prophecy of the coming of Jesus Christ. Satan has always been characterized as a serpent. Jesus Christ freed mankind from the bondage of sin at Calvary and defeated Satan forever. Satan has been crushed!

7. The serpent shall fight and lose the woman's seed (Genesis 3:15). Jesus Christ was of the seed of a woman, which was Mary. The woman's seed fought and overcame the serpent, which is Satan.

8. The woman will have painful childbearing (Genesis 3:16). When Adam and Eve were expelled from the Garden of Eden, they began producing children. As any woman will tell you, it is a very painful experience birthing a child.

9. The woman's desire will be for her husband (Genesis 3:16). While Adam and Eve were in the Garden of Eden, they lived together in harmony with God. They were not married to each other, and they had a platonic relationship. Adam and Eve both lived for God together and equality. After the expulsion from Eden, Eve had to depend not on God, but now she depended on Adam for most of her needs. Women's desire now was for their husbands instead on God.

10. The woman loses her independence (Genesis 3:16). While Adam and Eve were in the Garden of Eden, they were both equal to one another. After the expulsion Eve depended on Adam for food and shelter and protection. Life was easy in Eden. From now on life for both of them is much more difficult. Women from now on are much more dependent on their men.

11. The ground is cursed (Genesis 3: 17). In the Garden of Eden, the land was rich and fertile all of the time. Weeds and thistles never grew; only good thing to eat grew in abundance. Life was easy. All Adam and Eve had to do was to pick and eat and be full. After the expulsion from Eden life was much more difficult. Weed grew instead of vegetables. Thistles grew in abundance instead of fruit.

12. Adam must eat from the field (Genesis 3:19). If man wanted to eat from now on Adam will have to plant the crops and eat whatever he could grow. Sometimes the crops would grow and sometimes they would not grow.

13. Adam must work (Genesis 3:19). As any farmer will tell you crops do not grow by themselves! They have to be planted by hand, weeded, fertilized; birds and small animals need to be run off. Then the crops need to be harvested. They do not pick themselves and just jump into the bucket. Adam had to do all of this himself and work for his living.

14. Adam will die and return to the cursed ground (Genesis 3:19). Adam and Eve had eternal life. They did not grow old and did not die. That is now over! Now we live a short life and die. Our dead bodies are then buried in the ground. The bodies then rote and break apart and return back unto the earth.

Noah's Covenant: This covenant is located in Genesis 8:20- 9:17. This covenant is unconditional to man. This covenant does have a sign that we all know and love. The rainbow we see

64

after a good rain. It is current from the Flood unto the end of the current world. So, it is still in force today.

"And Noah builded an alter unto the Lord; and took of every clean beast, and of every clean fowl, and offered burnt offerings on the alter."

"And the Lord smelled a sweet savour; and the Lord said in His heart, I will not again curse the ground any more for man's sake; for the imagination of man's heart is evil from his youth; neither will I again smite any more everything living, as I have done."

"While the earth remaineth, seed time and harvest, and cold and heat, and summer and winter, and day and night shall not cease."

"And God blessed Noah and his sons, and said unto them, Be fruitful, and multiply, and replenish the earth."

"And the fear of you and the dread of you shall be upon every beast of the earth, and upon every fowl of the air, upon all that moveth upon the earth, and upon all the fishes of the sea; into your hand are they delivered."

"Every moving thing that liveth shall be meat for you; even as the green herb have, I given you all things."

"But flesh with the life thereof, which is the blood thereof, shall ye not eat."

"And surely your blood of your lives will I require; at the hand of every beast will I require it, and at the hand of every man; at the hand of every man's brother will I require the life of man."

"Whoso sheddeth man's blood, by man shall his blood be shed: for the image of God made He man."

"And you, be ye fruitful, and multiply; bring forth abundantly in the earth, and multiply therein."

"And God spake unto Noah, and to his sons with him, saying,"

"And I, behold, I establish my covenant with you, and with your seed after you;"

"And with every living creature that is with you, of the fowl, of the cattle, and of every living beast of the earth with you; from all that go out of the ark, to every beast of the earth."

"And God said, this is the token of the covenant which I make between Me and you and every living creature that is with you, for perpetual generations:"

I do set My bow in the cloud, and it shall be for a token of a covenant between Me and the earth."

And it shall come to pass, when I bring a cloud over the earth, that the bow shall be seen in the cloud:"

"And I will remember my covenant, which is between Me and you, and every living creature of all flesh; and the waters shall no more become a flood to destroy all flesh."

" And the bow shall be in the cloud; and I shall look upon it, that I may remember the everlasting covenant between God and every living creature of all flesh that is upon the earth."

"And God said unto Noah, this is the token of the covenant, which I have established between Me and all flesh that is upon all the earth."

Here are the contents and requirements of Noah's covenant.

1. God vowed never to curse the ground (Genesis 8:20-21). The first thing that Noah did when he left the ark was to set up an alter to the Lord and make a sacrifice. Noah was thankful and had

a good heart towards God. So, God vowed never to curse the ground (flooding) again.

2. God vowed never to kill all living creatures again (Genesis 8: 21). Just because man's heart is evil from his youth, why should all other creatures die? From now on man will be judged for his own sins.

3. God commanded Noah and his sons to have a lot of children (Genesis 9:1). God blessed Noah and his family and commanded them to multiply. God did not say to add to themselves, but to multiply! This is the same command God gave Adam and Eve in Genesis 1:28. This command has never been changed or countermanded. It is for us even today!

4. The fear of man was put into all animals (Genesis 9:2). As any biologist will confess, all animals have an instinctive fear of mankind. Why is this? The Flood.

5. All animals are delivered into our hands (Genesis 9:2). Mankind has the mental capacity to kill or capture all and any animal on this planet.

6. All animals as well plants are food (Genesis 9:3). God told Adam that they can eat all plant life for food. Now God is adding all animal life (except with the blood) to our diet. For the Israelite God will add some restrictions to this, but that will only apply to the Jews during the Law of Moses. But for non-Jews there have never been any restrictions since this time.

7. No one may eat blood (Genesis 9:4). We are forbidden to eat blood. Blood is to be shed for a sacrifice and not to be eaten (Acts 15). Christ would shed His Blood for the redemption of our sins. Blood is an important symbol and is not to be cheapened.

8. We may not murder our fellow man (Genesis 9:5-6). If we murder man we will be murdered by man. In other words, we will reap what we will sow. This also established the principle of

Capital Punishment; God will no longer deal with murders, but no man will police himself.

9. God will never flood the earth again Genesis 9:11-17). The rainbow is the sign of the covenant. Every time it rains, and the rainbow comes out, God looks upon it and remembers His covenant with all living things to never flood the earth again.

Figure 15: Abraham

Abraham's Covenant: This covenant is located in Genesis 12:1-3. But God clarifies this covenant three more times in 13:14-17; 15:1-18; 17:1-8. This is a conditional covenant for Abram, He had to be obedient and leave to this new land. The animal sacrifice in Genesis 15:8-15 and walking between them was the ancient way to seal an everlasting agreement. Today we get a lawyer and sign paper contracts. Back then it was much more personal. Abraham fell asleep (Genesis 15:12) and it was only God who walked between the animal sacrifice. This is because God vowed to protect and take care of Abrams future descendants, but He did not want to confuse Abram of future events.

This covenant does have a sign that was added later to the covenant. The sign is circumcision of all males on the eighth day. This sets them apart as a marked people. It was a mark of separation, purity, and possession. This sign is located in Genesis 17:9-14.

This covenant concludes when this world is over and until the new heavens and new earth is made. Here is Abram's Covenant as written in Genesis 12:1-3. So, it is still in force today.

> *"Now the Lord had said unto Abram, Get thee out of thy country, and from thy kindred, and from thy father's house, unto a land that I will shew thee:"*

> *"And I will make of thee a great nation, and I will bless thee, and make thy name great; and thou shalt be a blessing:"*

> *"And I will bless them that bless thee, and curse him that curseth thee: and in the shall all families of the earth be blessed."*

1. Leave your country (Genesis 12:1). God told Abram to leave his nation and people. He needed to give up the protection that a country can supply its people. From now on if Abram gets into trouble he will not have an entire nation to protect him. God asked Abram to leave all this and just rely on Him alone.

2. Leave your extended family (Genesis 12:1). Unlike American families, these families stayed together in one area. A family would grow, ten to twenty children per woman, and would stay in the same village, town, or area. Sometimes they would eventually form a tribe or even a nation. This family network would provide jobs and work for everyone. God asked Abram to abandon this network and to rely on Him alone.

3. Leave your father's house (Genesis 12:1). The father here meaning, family patriarch. It is the family patriarch that provided direct protection and financial assistance to the immediate

69

family. He was called father because almost always the family patriarch was the oldest male in the immediate family. God is in effect telling Abram that He will be his direct protector.

4. I will give you land (Genesis 12:1; 13:14-17; 17:8). No promise could be more meaningful than that of land and children in that day. This was a big promise to Abram. Even though the land was empty in that day it is very doubtful that Abram owned anything. Land was seldom owned, but controlled by the family patriarch or tribal leader. If they were nomadic then no one owned anything. This promise was a big reward for the faith Abram would need to fulfill the first three requites by the Lord.

5. I will give you a lot of descendants (Genesis 12:2; 13:16; 15:5; 17:2, 4-8). As before, no promise could be more meaningful than that of land and children in that day. In that day children meant security in old age. It could even mean your very survival. It also was a sign from God that you are blessed, and you are walking rightly before Him. This last belief is of course incorrect, but nevertheless, that was the widespread belief.

6. I will bless you (Genesis 12:2). God promised Abram that He would bless him. To have God bless the works of your hands is a very comforting promise. It means guaranteed prosperity. Today Abraham's name is only next to the name of Jesus Christ, and occurs some three-hundred times in Scripture.

7. I will make you a great man (Genesis 12:2). God said no matter what happens or were I lead you; you will be greatly respected by the people around you. Men need and crave respect. It is an important part of being a man. God promises Abram respect and honor in life.

8. You will be a blessing (Genesis 12:2). In Abram's mind this meant that God would make him a family patriarch. And indeed, he most certainly was a great patriarch. The family patriarch was the one who controlled all of the money and land and he did all of the blessing that was bestowed on others.

9. Abrams friends will be blessed, and his enemies will be cursed (Genesis 12:3). Other nations are mentioned throughout Scripture only when they come in contact with the Israelites. England and America have traditionally welcomed and protected the Jews and have been blessed accordingly. Europe has traditionally cursed the Jews and has been plagued with wars and disease.

10. All families of the earth will be blessed through you (Genesis 12:3). This is in reference to the coming Messiah, Jesus Christ, the redeemer of all mankind. In Christ all of the inhabitants of the earth have been blessed. Jesus Christ is a descendant of Abram both through the mother, Mary (Luke 3: 23-38), and Joseph (Matthew 1:1-17). The blessing is access to God through faith and eternal salvation by the name of all names, Jesus Christ.

Figure 16: Moses

Moses' Covenant (Law of Moses): As Abraham was the father of a people, Mosses' was the founder of the nation. Mosses' Covenant was given to the Israelite through Mosses. When Mosses discovered that he was a Hebrew, he decided to worship the God of the Hebrews. This meant giving up his life of privilege, and honor, and wealth to live like a slave with his people. Moses' Covenant is also called the "Law of Moses."

This covenant is located in Exodus 20:17-23:19; 25:1-40; 38; Leviticus 11-15; 17-20. This covenant is very large in comparison to all of the former covenants therefore I will outline it differently.

Moses' covenant is a conditional covenant for man. There is a promise of blessing if the Law is obeyed (Exodus 19:5-6; Leviticus 26:3; Deuteronomy 28:1-4, 29:9). But there is a promise of judgment if Israel did not obey (Leviticus 26:14-26; Deuteronomy 11:10-17, 28:15-68).

This Covenant has a sign, the Sabbath Day. This sign was given to the nation of Israel before the Advent of Christ, not to Gentiles or Christians (Romans 2:12-14; Exodus 20:12,20; 31:12-18; Deuteronomy 5:12-15). The Sabbath was part of the Law of Moses which was done away with in Christ. Christ did not change the Sabbath, but it just passed away with the Law of Moses. Moses' Covenant concluded with the coming of Christ (Galatians 3:19). The Sabbath to the Jews was a day of rest. Today we rest in a Person, Jesus Christ, not a day.

Moral Laws. These are the Ten Commandments. They are located in Exodus 20:1-17 and is repeated in Deuteronomy 5:1-22. Without obeying these ten laws all of the others are powerless! Nine of these ten laws are eternal laws and are still in effect today. Only the law to keep the Sabbath has been discontinued at Calvary.

Civil Laws: These were laws to govern the social life of Israel. These laws are found in Exodus 21-23; Leviticus 11-15, 17-20. These include laws governing slaves, Exodus 21:1-11. Buying and letting go free, slave children, and volunteering for slavery.

Laws about violent acts, Exodus 21:12-27. Murder, striking your parents, stealing slaves, cursing your parents, fighting, striking slaves, striking pregnant women, and bodily damage.

The responsibilities of owners of oxen, Exodus 21:28-36. If your ox kills another, damage done to an ox or by an ox. Laws about the repayment of stolen animals, Exodus 22:1-15. Repayment and restitution, damages.

Assorted moral and religious laws, Exodus 22:16- 23:9. Sex crimes, witches, bestiality, idolatry, treatment of strangers, widows, lending money.

Sabbatical day and year, Exodus 23:10-14. Letting the poor eat, no working.

The three great festivals, Exodus 23:14-19. The feasts of unleavened bread, harvest, and in gathering.

Animals that may be eaten, Leviticus 11. Which animals were clean or unclean for eating.

The Purification of woman after childbirth, Leviticus 12. Ceremonies for women after childbirth.

Laws concerning skin diseases, Leviticus 13:1-46. Different ways to spot leprosy.

Laws concerning mildew, Leviticus 13:47-59. Cleaning and burning items with mildew.

Purification after having skin diseases, Leviticus 14:1-32. Sacrifice and ceremony.

Mildew in houses, Leviticus 14:33-57. Cleaning and repairing houses with mildew.

Unclean bodily discharges, Leviticus 15. Washing everything that is touched by mochas, blood or puss.

The sacredness of blood, Leviticus 17. Laws concerning blood of people and animals.

Forbidden sexual practices, Leviticus 18. Public nudity, adultery, sacrificing children, and homosexuality.

Laws of holiness and justice, Leviticus 19. Holiness, idolatry, offerings, gleanings for the poor, stealing, sex, swearing, treatment of workers, deaf and blind, respect of persons, gossiping, hating, revenge, unclean breeding, sex with slaves, fruit trees, eating blood, witchcraft, cutting hair, tattoos, prostitution, wizards, and treatment of strangers.

Penalties for disobedience, Leviticus 20. Sixteen laws that required the death penalty.

Ceremonial Laws: These are laws to govern the religious life of Israel. These laws are found in Exodus 25:1-40; 38.

The Ark, Exodus 25: 10-22. Measurements and materials in its construction.

The table for a bread offering, Exodus 25: 23-30. Measurements and materials in its construction.

The Lamp Stand, Exodus 25: 31-40. Measurements and materials in its construction.

The Tabernacle, Exodus 26 Measurements and materials in its construction.

The Alter, Exodus 27: 1-8. Measurements and materials in its construction.

The Court of the Tabernacle, Exodus 27: 9-19. Measurements and materials in its construction.

Taking care of the Lamp, Exodus 27: 20-21. Oil and operation.

The Garments for the Priests, Exodus 28: 1-14. Who wore these garments and why? Which materials were used to make them?

The Breastplate, Exodus 28: 15-30. Measurements and materials in its construction.

The other priestly garments, Exodus 28: 31-43. Measurements and materials and engravings and who wore them.

Instructions for ordaining Aaron and his sons as priests, Exodus 29: 1-37, and wave offering and ceremony with anointing.

Daily offerings, Exodus 29: 38-46. Lamb offerings in the morning and evening.

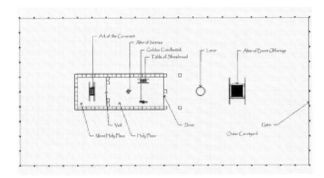

Figure 17: The Tabernacle

Altar for burning incense, Exodus 30: 1-10. Measurements and materials in it' construction. When to burn incense.

Tax for the Tabernacle, Exodus 30: 11-16. Half a shekel from every person.

Bronze Basin, Exodus 30: 17-21. Where to put it.

Anointing Oil, Exodus 30: 22-33. Recipe for the oil and how to use it.

Incense, Exodus 30: 34-38. Recipe to make it.

Sabbath Day, Exodus 31:12-18. Penalty for defiling, a sign.

Day of Atonement, Leviticus 16:1-19; 23:26-32. Sin and burnt offering, sacrifices, scapegoat, and the ceremony.

The Scapegoat, Leviticus 16:20-28. Putting sins upon it and setting the goat free, then themselves washing.

Observing the Day of Atonement, Leviticus 16:29-34. When and why.

The holiness of the priests, Leviticus 21. They and their families must live a holy lifestyle, and the penalty for disobedience.

The holiness of the offerings, Leviticus 22. Keeping it ceremonial clean and inspection of sacrificial animals.

The religious festivals, Leviticus 23:1-4. Proclaims the Sabbath then introduces the rest.

Passover and unleavened bread, Leviticus 23:5-14. The fourteenth day of the first month, seven days celebration. Education. Wave, lamb and meat offerings. No working.

Harvest festival, Leviticus 23:15-22. Time of the year. Meat, wave, burnt, and drink offerings. Sacrifices. Gleanings for the poor. No working.

New year festival, Leviticus 23:23-25. Time of the year, no working.

Festival of Tabernacles, Leviticus 23:33-44. Time of the year, seven days. Gifts and vows. Living in booths.

Taking care of the Lamps, Leviticus 24:1-4. Oil and location.

The bread offered to God, Leviticus 24:5-9. Cake ceremony with the priests eating them.

An example of just and fair punishment, Leviticus 24:10-23. God uses a situation to set an example for all Israel.

The seventh year Sabbath, Leviticus 25:1-7; 18-22. No farming to let the land rest for a year.

The year of Jubilee, this has also been called the year of Restoration, Leviticus 25:8-17; 23-34. No farming for a year. Returning land and possessions to their original owners. Freeing Jewish slaves.

Loans for the poor, Leviticus 25:35-38. No usury was to be charged.

Release of slaves, Leviticus 25:39-55. Take no Jewish slaves, but pay them to work until the year of Jubilee. Keeping foreign slaves. A rich foreigner that sells a poor Jew into slavery can be redeemed by a relative.

Blessings of obedience, Leviticus 26:1-13. Rain in season, land will increase, plenty of food, safety and peace, victory in battle, many children.

Punishment of disobedience, Leviticus 26:14-46. Disease, heartbreak, famine and drought, defeat in battle and occupation, wild beasts will kill children and animals, scattered among the heathen.

Laws concerning gifts to the Lord, Leviticus 27. Making vows of money unto the Lord. The priests shall estimate persons or property.

David's Covenant: This covenant is located in 2 Samuel 7:8-19. David's Covenant was made with David, thru the prophet Nathan, five-hundred years after the era of Moses. This covenant was made by God and is unconditional and eternal (2 Samuel 7:14). This Covenant has a sign in Luke 2:11-12, "For unto you is born this day, in the city of David, a savior, which…." The covenant is in two parts. The first part is what God has already done for David. The second part is what God will do for David. Here is the covenant.

"I took thee from the sheepcote, from following the sheep, to be ruler over my people, over Israel:"

"And I was with thee whithersoever thou wentest, and have cut off all thine enemies out of thy sight, and have made thee a great name, like unto the name of the great men that are in the earth."

"Moreover, I will appoint a place for my people Israel, and will plant them, that they may dwell in a place of their own, and move no more; neither shall the children of wickedness afflict them any more, as beforetime,"

" And as since the time that I commanded judges to be over my people Israel, and have caused thee to rest from all thine enemies. Also the Lord telleth thee that he will make thee an house."

"And when thy days be fulfilled, and thou shalt sleep with thy fathers, I will set up thy seed after thee, which shall proceed out of thy bowels, and I will establish his kingdom."

"He shall build an house for my name, and I will stablish the throne of his kingdom forever. I will be his father, and he shall be my son. If he commits iniquity, I will chasten him with the rod of men, and with the stripes of the children of men:"

"But my mercy shall not depart away from him, as I took it away from Saul, whom I put away before thee."

"And thine house and thy kingdom shall be established for ever before thee: thy throne shall be established forever."

What God has already done:

1. I took you from the sheepcote (2 Samuel 7:8). A sheepcote is a very small, temporary shelter for sheep. God reminds David of his very humble origin in which God has called David from. Shepherd's like David had to sleep at night with his sheep in such a shelter. Just in case it is all starting to go to David's head!

2. *I made you ruler over Israel (2 Samuel 7:8).* Just a little reminder that it was really God that has installed David to the throne of Israel. God was working behind the scenes to make it all happen.

3. I was with you (2 Samuel 7:9). God has placed his Spirit upon David (Psalm 51:11). God was with David the entire time of his journey to the throne of Israel. Just like today, without the Spirit of God in our lives we can do nothing.

4. I defeated your enemies (2 Samuel 7:9). It was really God the whole time that directed the fighting. David had been outnumbered the whole time.

5. I made you a great man (2 Samuel 7:9). Clearly, without the Holy Spirit David would not have achieved so much. And this had given David a great name among the people.

6. I will appoint a place for Israel (2 Samuel 7:10). The people will remain in the Promised Land by the hand of God. They are there today.

What God will do:

7. The wicked will not afflict Israel (2 Samuel 7:10). As long as they stay obedient, God will not let other people's hurt or dominate the people of Israel. Israel stayed the dominate power in that are for the next eighty years.

8. I will make your descendants rulers of Israel (2 Samuel 7:11-12). David's descendants will continue to rule over Israel, as long as they remain obedient. Jesus Christ is a direct descendant of David.

9. Your son will build God's Temple (2 Samuel 7:13). King Solomon did in fact build the Temple. David collected the material's ad Solomon had it built.

10. Your throne will be eternal (2 Samuel 7:13,16). Jesus Christ is the descendant of David through his father and mother. Jesus Christ is eternal, so the throne of David is eternal.

11. God will have a close relationship with David's descendants (2 Samuel 7:14). This is historically correct. God did work with the following king's after David.

12. Their sin will be punished by man (2 Samuel 7:14). God uses man to do His will. This is the case with most things.

13. God's Mercy will never be taken away from David's descendants (2 Samuel 7:15). We still have it today though the mercy and grace of Jesus Christ!

Figure 18: The New Covenant

The New Covenant: This Covenant is located in Jeremiah 31:31-34. It is later fulfilled in Acts 2, and explained in Hebrews 7-9. It has no conditions and is eternal. The covenant began in Acts 2 and is here today. Here is the New Covenant.

> *"Behold, the days come, saith the LORD, that I will make a new covenant with the house of Israel, and with the house of Judah:"*

> *"Not according to the covenant that I made with their fathers in the day that I took them by the hand to bring them out of the land of Egypt; which my covenant they brake, although I was an husband unto them, saith the LORD:"*

> *"But this shall be the covenant that I will make with the house of Israel; After those days, saith the LORD, I will put my law in their inward parts, and write it in their hearts; and will be their God, and they shall be my people."*

> *"And they shall teach no more every man his neighbor, and every man his brother, saying, Know the LORD: for they shall all know me, from the least of them unto the greatest of them, saith the LORD: for I will forgive their iniquity, and I will remember their sin no more."*

This is the great promise from God to Israel of a coming New Covenant that will be much greater than Moses' Covenant that the Israelis just could not keep. Even though this covenant was promised to the Jews, God had promised from the very beginning that He was going to graft into Israel, the Gentile nations (Exodus 4:22; Hosea 11: 1). Later, when the New Covenant was created, they were grafted into this new Kingdom (Romans 9:4; 2 Corinthians 6:18; James 1:18).

This prophecy was made to Israel by the mouth of Jeremiah only a few short years before the Jews are taken away into captivity in about 606bc. The people know was coming, but they would not repent to the LORD of their sins if disobedience. Jeremiah gave some of the Jews hope of a coming day of salvation in the midst of their dire situation. Here is the promise that was spoken by Jeremiah.

1. A future covenant (Jeremiah 31:31). This covenant will not be now, but in the future. "...the days come..." Jeremiah is very clear that this is a prophecy of the future. It was prepared by Christ and began upon His death on the cross, and was fulfilled in Acts 2.

2. This covenant is with the Jews (Jeremiah 31:31). It is clear that this covenant is with the house of Israel and Judah. But remember Christians have been grafted into these houses.

3. A new covenant (Jeremiah 31:32). This is not Moses' Covenant or a continuation of the same. This will be a completely new covenant.

4. Holy Spirit (Jeremiah 31:33). God said that He would put this new law into our hearts and our inward parts. Later in Acts 2 we see the fulfillment of this with the coming of the Holy Spirit in the lives of Christians.

5. They shall know me (Jeremiah 31:34). Everyone today knows who the LORD is and is all about. In Jeremiah's time this was not the case. Only Jews, or someone who knew a Jew understood their God. Today everyone knows the LORD. But we Christians know Him in a deeper way upon receiving the Holy Spirit. We read the Word to learn of Him, but to know God is to be filled with His Spirit.

The covenant of Moses, or the Law of Moses, is now obsolete now that Christ has come (Hebrews 8:13). It has been made obsolete because Christ has made a better covenant with us (Hebrews 7:19; 8:6-7). Moses' Covenant originated on earth in Mt. Sinai (Galatians 4:24-25), but the New Covenant originated in heaven from New Jerusalem above (Galatians 4:26-27). Moses' Covenant was totally impossible to obey (Romans 8:3) and brought nothing but death and condemnation (2 Corinthians 3:7-9). But the

New Covenant brings life (Ephesians 2:1-13) and was fulfilled perfectly by Christ (Luke 22:20; 1 Corinthians 11:25). Moses' Covenant they were required to bring annul atonement for their sins (Hebrews 9:7-8; 10:1-4) and this restricted their access to God (Hebrews 9:7-8). But the New Covenant removed sin once and for all in our lives (Hebrews 9:12; 10:2,22) and opened up our access to God (Hebrews 9:15-16).

Cultural Gap Principle

The Cultural Gap Principle is where our culture is different from the story in the text. By not understanding the different cultures involved throughout the Bible we can become confused and take the text out of context.

There are hundreds of different nations around the world, and many of these nations have many different languages and subcultures within them. Because the Bible was written in Roman empire and Israel, we must understand the Bible in their cultural context.

Genesis 14:18-19: *"And Melchizedek king of Salem brought forth bread and wine: and he was the priest of the most high God. And he blessed him, and said, blessed be Abram of the most high God, possessor of heaven and earth."*

In order to understand this story of the Bible, the Bible student must understand the customs of the day. Those customs are very much different than it is today.

In chapter fourteen of the book of Genesis it tells the story of four kings led by a king named Chedorlaomer. They attacked five kings in the valley of Siddim. In today's world that would seem unreasonable and illegal. What we need to understand is that in that day it was normal! Kings in that day went to war in order to collect loot and prestige. When Abram's nephew Lot was taken captive, Abram was duty bound to come to his rescue and meet out some level of revenge.

Abram pursued these four kings and soundly defeated them. According to the times of that day, Abram had the right to all of the loot that was taken from the raid of the valley of Siddim. That would be unheard of today. In that day it was the norm.

There is an old saying, "everyone has a boss." And Abram had a boss. God may had promised all of this land to Abram, but he did not control the land. The king in charge of that area of land was the king of Salem, Melchizedek. In that day the man in charge had the right to ten percent of any spoils. Today this would be unheard of and illegal by international law.

In order for the Bible student to understand this story we must understand the customs of that day, and how those folks thought. If we can put ourselves in their shoes then we can understand the story much better. This is a cultural gap we need to cross and understand.

Figure 19: Genesis, the beginning

Genesis 47:13-26: *"And Joseph bought all the land of Egypt for Pharaoh; for the Egyptians sold every man his field, because the famine prevailed over them: so, the land became Pharaoh's. And as for the people, he removed them to cities from one end of the borders of Egypt even to the other end thereof."* *(Genesis 47:20-21).*

These verses are set up by the happenings in chapter forty-one. Let me set up the context. In chapter forty-one Joseph is given a dream from God about an upcoming seven years of plenty and then seven years of famine!

Chapter forty-two through chapter forty-six we have the story of Jacob and his family coming to Egypt and getting settled in. In chapter forty-seven we get into the seven years of famine.

There were no farmer co-ops back in those days so the Egyptian government would buy the grain and cattle and sell it domestically or ship it to foreign lands.

As the famine continued, the people of Egypt bought grain from the government (Joseph). Then they sold their cattle. Then they sold themselves into slavery for food. Remember, the government had all of the grain!

What the Bible student needs to understand is that that was the normal way of doing things in that day. Today that would be unheard of! Selling oneself to the government into slavery for food that was all controlled by the government would never happen! But in that day, it was normal and the slavery institution itself was considered normal. That is a very large cultural gap from that day to today.

Ruth 3:9: *"And he said, Who art thou? And she answered, I am Ruth thine handmaid: spread therefore thy skirt over thine handmaid; for thou art a near kinsmen."*

If we can put the subject of the kinsman redeemer aside this time. The reason I am using this example is the fact that Ruth is asking Boaz to cover her in his skirt.

Men for thousands of years wore dresses and skirts! They wore them for freedom of movement of their legs. This is especially so for Roman and Greek soldiers. These soldiers wore skirts for the freedom of movement in hand combat reasons.

Dresses and skirts were wearing by both men and woman and both genders had a different design. The Bible student today needs to understand this rather large cultural gap! The standard of dress is very different in different cultural today and most especially in ancient times. Those differences are not wrong, just different.

Nehemiah 2:2: "Wherefore *the king said unto me, why is thy countenance sad, seeing thou art not sick? This is nothing else but sorrow of heart. Then I was very sore afraid.*"

Figure 20: Ruins of Jerusalem

Why would Nehemiah be afraid? And not just afraid, but "sore afraid." That means in today's English that he was terrified! Well, in that day and culture, servants of the king had to be happy and have a big smile, for the king's pleasure. The king and the royal family did not want to have servants with sad and long faces. They were therefore to have a happy face and attitude under the pain of death if they did not. Nehemiah was so concerned about Jerusalem's run-down condition that he slipped up and had a sad face around the king.   So, Nehemiah feared death for this simple mistake! Unthinkable today but a real fear in that day.

Mark 7:11-13: *"For Moses said, Honour thy father and thy mother; and, whoso curseth father or mother, let him die the death:"*

"But ye say, if a man shall say to his father or mother, it is Corban, that is to say, a gift, by whatsoever thou mightiest be profited by me; he shall be free, And ye suffer him no more to do aught for his father or his mother; Making the word of God of none effect through your tradition, which ye have delivered: and many such things do ye."

Jesus upbraids the Pharisees soundly for their concept of Corban. In the practice of Corban, a man could declare that all his money would go to the temple treasury when he died, and that, since his money belonged to God, he was therefore no longer responsible for maintaining his aging parents. Jesus argues that men were using this Pharisaic tradition to render God's command (the fifth commandment) of no account. Without a knowledge of the cultural practice of Corban, we would be unable to understand this passage.[7]

The reason why Pharisees went along with that practice is that they received a monetary bribe in order for him to declare a Corban. The priest's had access to all of the temple's money and they took bribes on the side to make more. The preachers of that day loved their money as some still do today. The priest's and scribes were guilty of placing human tradition and their own greed above divine revelation.

---

[7] Bullinger, Ethelbert, William. *Figures of Speech in the Bible.* Baker Book House, Grand Rapids, MI. 1897.

Figure 21: The Apostles

Dispensation Principle

A dispensation, or administration, is a period of time in which God deals with man's sin and man's responsibility to that sin. The Bible student must understand this principle or else the Bible will be a book of confusion and contradiction. If this principle is ignored then Scripture will be misinterpreted. The Apostle Paul understood that a part of a dispensation had been committed to him (1 Corinthians 9:17).

To give an example: Abraham was made righteous by his faith in the promises of God, not by his faith in Jesus Christ. That is because Abraham did not know anything about the coming Christ. Therefore, his salvation cannot be judged by New Testament standards of faith and salvation. God dealt with Abraham according to his dispensation of time and us in ours. There are seven dispensations.

Dispensation of Innocence: This time is from creation to the fall of Adam and Eve. Adam and Eve begin this time blameless before God, but end it as sinners (Genesis 1:26-2:23). The number of years that this was unknown. It is called the time of innocence because there was no sin upon the earth or man.

Man's responsibility was to be obedient to God's Word. Adam and Eve had been given instructions by God but did not understand the concept of good or evil. They were confronted with a choice; Obey God's Word or listens to Satan. Man chose to listen to Satan rather than God. Adam and Eve had only one rule, and that was not to eat of the tree of good and evil, (Genesis 2:17). Satan convinced Eve to eat of the forbidden tree in the midst of the garden.

The consequence of failure was his banishment from the garden of Eden, pain in childbirth and loss of authority for the woman. Sin had destroyed the world that they knew.

God showed mercy to them by giving them a Messianic promise of victory over Satan in the future.

"And I will put enmity between thee and the woman, and between thy seed and her seed; it shall bruise thy head, and thou shalt bruise his head." (Genesis 3:15).

Dispensation of Conscience: This time period is from the fall of Adam and Eve to the Flood; this was about sixteen-hundred years and is located in Genesis 3-7. Mankind is now in a fallen sinful condition and now has a limit to his life. Mankind's responsibility is now to choose between good or evil and to worship and sacrifice to God (Genesis 4:7).

Abel chooses the good, but Cain chooses the evil. Mankind slowly grew wicked and chose evil until all were evil except one family. Mankind had become so wicked that God's only consideration was to destroy the entire earth. The dispensation starts with the rebellion of Cain in his bloodless sacrifice and ends with God showing divine mercy to eight obedient people with some animals (Genesis 7:1).

Dispensation of Human Government: This time period begins after the Flood with Noah and his family, and ends at the destruction of the Tower of Babel (Genesis 8-11). This was about four-hundred years. Mankind was to govern them, but failed.

Noah and his descendant's responsibility were to worship and sacrifice to God and to choose good over evil. It starts out well but evil begins within a few years with the alcohol abuse of Noah and Canaan's response and judgment. If man cannot rule his own life righteously how could he rule other people? This shows mankind that he needs a savior to save him from his sinful condition! After this mankind slips further into evil and had been scattered by an act of God with the confusion of languages and the destruction of the Tower of Babel.

God had blessed this people with abundance of food and water and shelter, since the people had plenty of time to build the massive tower. They could only have done this if they had plenty of free time for building. The dispensation ends with divine mercy from God in allowing the people to live and prosper even though they all have given themselves over to idolatry. God decides to look for another man who can begin again. This looks to the future, where God will begin again in Christ, to start the Church. The next two dispensations are for the Jewish people only, the rest of the world still stayed in this dispensation. So, for the next two-thousand years the world had two dispensations at the same time.

Dispensation of Promise: This time is from the Call of Abraham to the Mt. Sinai. This dispensation lasted about four-hundred thirty years, and it was only for the Jewish people. It can be found in Genesis 11-15. Abraham probably lived in idolatry at the time, but God had seen something in him. Abraham became righteous in God's eyes when he believed God's promises.

Mankind's responsibility was to live in the Promised Land and to claim it, worship and sacrifice to God. Mankind failed in this responsibility when Jacob's family all settled in Egypt during a severe famine (Genesis 47:1) and had fallen into idolatry (Ezekiel 20:7-9).

The end result of this failure was God's chosen people became slaves to a wicked nation (Exodus 1). But God had Mercy on them and delivered them from bondage. God had decided to continue to work with this family. This shows us today that even if we fall back into spiritual bondage God will continue to work to make us better.

Dispensation of Law: This time is from Mt. Sinai to Calvary. This was about fifteen-hundred years in length, and it was for the Jewish people only. It begins with God leading the Israelite out of spiritual and physical bondage and ends with the temporary rejection of Judaism for Christianity and the Church.

93

These Laws were given to the Jewish people only (Romans 2:12; 9:4). Their responsibility was to keep the Law of Moses (Exodus 19:5). Not only did the Jewish people fail to keep the Law (2 Kings 17:7-17; Acts 2:22-23), but the only man who ever did, they are quickly and without regret tortured and executed that man. Because of the Jews failure they were taken away into bondage into Assyria and Babylon (2 Kings 17:6; 25:11), then later scattered into the entire world.

God showed His Divine Mercy to the entire world by coming down in Christ, dying for mankind's sins, and providing the ultimate sacrifice Himself.

Figure 22: Dispensation of Promise

Dispensation of Grace: This dispensation time is from Calvary to the second coming of Christ. This dispensation time has lasted for over two-thousand years and continues on to the present. This is our age! At the start of this dispensation the world is united again in the same dispensation again. Jesus Christ was the sacrifice for the sins of all mankind. In this time all of our sins are forgiven in repentance, and washed away in baptism in the name of Jesus Christ, then comes the infilling of the Holy Spirit.

Mankind's responsibilities in this dispensation are to believe on Jesus Christ as God and to worship and live for Him. From now on there are only two classes of people in the world: saved sinners and lost sinners, all depending on our response to Christ. Mankind will ultimately fail and fall into unrepentant sin (1 Timothy 4:1-3; 2 Timothy 4:3-4).

God has shown His Divine Mercy for over two-thousand years. At the end of this dispensation Christ will return to rule and judge the world. Those who die will be lost forever, those who survive without Christ will live in the Kingdom age, believers will live in the New Jerusalem and help Christ rule the rest of the world.

Dispensation of God's Kingdom: This dispensation time is from the second coming of Christ to the Great White Judgment. This will be a one-thousand-year age. This is a future dispensation (Psalms 2 and 11). Mankind will be under the direct rule of Jesus Christ and His Kingdom (Acts 15:14-17); Psalm 2:6; Matthew 24:29-30; Isaiah 24:23).

Mankind's responsibility will be to worship King Jesus, be obedient to the Kingdom and to worship (Psalms 2:12; 67:4; 86:9; Isaiah 65:20; Zechariah 14:17. Mankind will ultimately be deceived by Satan and fail and be judged.

After one-thousand years mankind will rebel against God and march an army against His Kingdom (Psalm 66:3; Revelation 20:7-9). At which time fire coming down from God out of Heaven will destroy them (Revelation 20:9). The earth will be destroyed, and all the saved will be in Heaven for eternity.

Some had taught that there are eight different dispensations and that the additional one is the "Dispensation of Tribulation." They say that this one would last for seven years during the tribulation period. This is simply not correct since there is nothing in Scripture to prove the existence of this dispensation. Jesus did talk on a period of time He called the tribulation (Matthew 24:29-31). But how God deals with sin is the same as in the dispensation of Grace. We will still come to God through Acts 2:38 for salvation.

Summary of the Dispensations: In each dispensation the trend of man is away from God. The responsibility of man in each dispensation is to believe the Word of God and to obey Him. At the end of each dispensation, God gives man up to his own way.

Each dispensation shows that evil is headed up in a person or persons:

1. Dispensation of Innocence- Satan.
2. Dispensation Conscience- Sinful fallen angels.
3. Dispensation of Human Government- Nimrod.
4. Dispensation of Promise- Pharaoh.
5. Dispensation of Law- Scribes and Pharisees.
6. Dispensation of Grace- Modernists.
7. Dispensation of The Kingdom- Satan.

Each dispensation ends in a world crisis:

1. Dispensation of Innocence- Expulsion of man from the garden.
2. Dispensation of Conscience- The Flood.
3. Dispensation of Human Government- Confusion of Tongues.
4. Dispensation of Promise- Bondage.
5. Dispensation of Law- The Cross of Christ.
6. Dispensation of Grace- The Rapture of the Church.

7. Dispensation of Kingdom- Fire from Heaven.

In each dispensation God comes down:

1. Dispensation of Innocence- God came down to the garden.

2. Dispensation of Conscience- God talked with Noah.

3. Dispensation of Human Government "Let us go down."

4. Dispensation of Promise- "I am come down." (burning bush)

5. Dispensation of Law- Incarnation of Christ.

6. Dispensation of Grace- The Lord shall descend.

7. Dispensation of Kingdom- Still upon the earth.

Figure 23: Apostles

Double Reference Principle

This is a passage of prophetic Scripture which applies to a person or event near at hand, but is also a reference to the coming Christ. Two different times of fulfillment may also be referred to in one passage. Here are some examples.

Deuteronomy 18:15: *"The Lord thy God will raise up unto thee a Prophet from the midst of thee, of thy brethren, like unto me; unto him ye shall hearken."*

In this verse Moses was telling the people of Israel in his day that God was to raise up a prophet, like himself, in the near future. What he did not know was that he was also giving a double reference.

Moses's statement is concerning a prophet to follow him. The reference here is to Joshua (a type of Christ) and yet it looks forward to Christ also (Acts 3:22-23).

The Apostle Peter, here in the book of Acts, clearly points this out to the priests in the Temple that this prophecy was a double reference to Jesus Christ.

2 Samuel 7:12-16: *"...I will set up thy seed after thee, which shall proceed out of thy bowels, and I will establish his kingdom. He shall build an house for my name, and I will stablish the throne of his kingdom for ever."*

David's Covenant. It has to do with Solomon in one sentence, and the very next verse goes beyond to Christ. The psalmist in Psalm 132:11 would later reinforce this double reference.

Jeremiah 50-51: Predicted judgment on Babylon. It has not yet been completely fulfilled. There is double reference here to a future Babylon that will be destroyed in Revelation 18:9-21.

Ezekiel 36:24-28: In verse twenty-four it speaks of God bringing Israel back to the Promised Land from their exile in Babylon. *"For I will take you from among the heathen, and gather you out of all countries, and will bring you into your own land."*

Then, in verse twenty-seven, it turns to God giving His Spirit to man symbolizing a new promised land. *"And I will put my spirit within you, and cause you to walk in my statutes, and ye shall keep my judgments, and do them."* This came to pass in Acts 2:38 where God put His Spirit into man, a double reference that continues today!

Hosea 11:1: *"Out of Egypt have I called my son."* The Holy Spirit applies it to the experience of Christ when taken into Egypt and brought out in Matthew 2:14. The New Testament agrees that it is a double reference.

The birth of Christ- Isaiah 7:14-16: "A good example may be taken from Isaiah's prediction concerning a sign to be given to Ahaz. The sign was needed as a way of reassuring Ahaz that God would shortly deliver Jerusalem from a siege by the kings of Israel and Syria.

The prophet identified the sign as the birth of a child; before the child would know good from evil, the deliverance would be affected. This prophecy must have been fulfilled already in Ahaz' day for it to have been meaningful as a sign to him. This fulfillment is best identified with the birth of Isaiah's own son , Maher-shalal-hash-baz (Isaiah 8:1-4). This could not have been the complete fulfillment, however, because the child to be born would

100

be the child of a virgin, and his name would be called Emmanuel. This complete fulfillment came only with Christ, as Matthew 1:22-23 clearly states."[8]

[8] Wood Leon J. *The Bible and Future Events*. Zondervan Publishing House, Grand Rapids, MI., p. 25. 1973.

First Mention Principle

The first occurrence of a subject in Scripture. It usually holds the key to understanding the subject. The first time it is mentioned usually defines it's meaning throughout Scripture. Here are some examples.

Spirit of God- Genesis 1:2: "And the earth was without form, and void; and darkness was upon the face of the deep. And the Spirit of God moved upon the face of the waters."

It was the Spirit of God from the beginning who created the earth and everything in it. Evolution envisioned by man had nothing to do with it. The universe was supernaturally created by God. The Spirit of God and the Holy Spirit and Jesus Christ are all one as later told by the Apostle John in 1 John 1.

Holiness- Genesis- 2:3: *"And God blessed the seventh day, and sanctified it."* Sanctification is the act of making or becoming holy. Holiness is from the beginning, and it should also be in our lives.

Satan is a deceiver- Genesis 3: This entire chapter deals with the deception of the devil. The devil will slightly twist the Words of God to deceive. That is the pattern that we have from the very beginning of creation.

Temptation- Genesis 3:1-6: Satan's temptation of Eve can be conceptualized in six steps, steps that can be seen in Satan's temptation of believer's today.

1. Minimizing the restriction. Step one is found in the first verse. Satan said to the woman: *"Yea, hath God said, Ye shall* *not eat of every tree of the garden?"* Satan's ploy is rather obvious: he was getting Eve to take her eyes off all the things God had given her to enjoy, and to focus on the one thing that God had forbidden.

2. Minimizing the consequences. Satan minimized the consequences of sin in two ways: first, by telling Eve that the consequences of sin would not be as bad as they had been stated to be, and second, by eventually focusing her attention so completely on the tree that she forgot about the consequences entirely.

3. Relabeling the action: In verse five Satan deftly tried to remove his temptation from the category of sin by relabeling it. In this particular instance, partaking of the fruit was relabeled as a way of expanding her consciousness. She would become a more complete person if she tried it once. Before this time Eve had thought of the forbidden action as disobedience: now she sees it as a necessity if she is to become a complete and mature person. Mixing good and evil: C.S. Lewis has commented that evil is often a perversion of something good that God has created. In verse six Satan added potency to his temptation by mixing good with evil: Eve saw that the tree was good for food.

5. Mixing sin with beauty: Temptation often comes wrapped in the form of something beautiful, something that appeals to our senses and desires. It is often necessary to think twice before we recognize that a beautiful object or goal is really sin in disguise.

6. Misunderstanding the implications: Although this may seem like a less significant point in the temptation process, it is perhaps the most crucial. In effect, by accepting Satan's statement, Eve was calling God a liar, even though she might not have recognized those implications of her action. She accepted Satan as the truth-teller and God as the prevaricator: by partaking of the fruit she was implicitly stating her belief that Satan was more interested in her welfare than God was. Yielding to the temptation implied that she accepted Satan's analysis of the situation instead of God's.[9]

Babylon- Genesis 10:10: "And the beginning of his kingdom was Babel..." The city of Babylon was born in sin from the very beginning.

Faith- Genesis 15:6: *"And he believed in the Lord; and he counted it to him for righteousness."* Faith is probably the most important biblical topic, and here is the first mention of faith.

Jerusalem- Genesis 14:18: *"And Melchizedek king of Salem brought forth bread and wine: and he was the priest of the highest God.* Bread and wine are well known symbols of life and prosperity. It still is today.

Son of Man- Psalm 8:4: *"What is man, that thou art mindful of him? And the son of man, that thou visitest him?"* Jesus Christ will in the future refer to Himself as the son of man.

Day of the Lord- Isaiah 2:11,12: *"The lofty looks of man shall be humbled, and the haughtiness of men shall be bowed down, and the Lord alone shall be exalted in that day. For the day of the Lord of hosts shall be upon every one that is proud and lofty, and upon every one that is lifted up; and he shall be brought low."* This is prophecy about the Last Days that we read about in the Book of Revelation.

---

[9] Virkler, Henry A. *Hermeneutics: Principles and Processes of Biblical Interpretation.* Baker Book House, Grand Rapids, MI., ps. 218-219. 1981.

Figure 24: Starting

Four-Fold Principle

The Four-Fold Principle reflects God's four-fold nature in His Word. By understanding God's four-fold nature we will understand our own nature, which is also a four-fold nature since we are all made in God's own image. Here are some examples.

The Exodus: When it became obvious that Moses could not lead so many people alone, God gave Moses a four-fold leadership plan that reflected God's own nature.

1. Moses. Moses was the ultimate leader and the final decision maker. Every organization needs to have someone where the buck stops. That was the roll of Moses! Every family needs to have a Patriarch to make a final decision.

2. Aaron. Aaron was the leader of all the Levites and the Tabernacle. He was the religious leader of the Israelites. The father is the family priest, and he is the one to make the religious decisions of his family.

3. Levites. The Levites did all of the work of priests in the service of the Tabernacle. They did all of the work of Tabernacle service. All of us need to pray and attend church service and support the church.

4. Elders. The Elders made all of the small decisions for the people. They handled all of the secular, tribal, and personal issues with the people. The Patriarch of our families need to make any decision that cannot be resolved among the family members.

When Israel camped and rested for the night, they were guarded by the four primary tribes; Judah, Reuben, Ephraim, Dan. Four tribes of Israel.

The four trees of Israel- Judges 9:7-15: The four trees referred to- the Fig-tree, the Olive, the vine, and the Bramble- are the four which are used to combine the whole of Israel's history.

1. Fig- tree. The Fig-tree represents the *National position* of Israel, from which we learn (in the Synoptic Gospels) that it withered away and has been cut down.

2. Olive tree. The Olive tree represents the Covenant privileges of Israel (Romans 11): which are now in abeyance.

3. Vine. The vine represents Israel's *Spiritual blessings*, which henceforth are to be found only in Christ, the True Vine (John 15).

4. Bramble. The Bramble represents the Antichrist, in whose shadow they will yet trust, but who will be to Israel a consuming fire in the day of "Jacob's trouble"- "the great Tribulation."[10]

Ezekiel's vision: The prophet Ezekiel was active during the Babylonian captivity of the Jewish people. He had seen a vision. He had seen a whirlwind, and out of this whirlwind he saw the likeness of four living creatures. This was a picture of the nature of God and the nature of the coming Christ, who is God in the flesh. Well, that living creature had the likeness of a man (Ezekiel 1:5). Everyone had four faces and four wings (Ezekiel 1:6). They had four faces in four different directions. They each had a set of wings for each direction.

The four living creatures had four faces. The face of a man, lion, ox, and eagle.

These faces represent the four natures of God. Let's take a look at the four faces that Ezekiel had seen.

---

[10] Bullinger, Ethelbert William. *Figures of Speech used in the Bible*. Baker Book House, Grand Rapids, MI., ps. 749-750. 1897.

1. Man. This is the face of humanity. When Jesus Christ arrived, He was God, but He was also at the same time a man. He loved, He cried, He hurt, He felt hardship. He felt and experienced all of the emotions we feel every day. God set the ultimate example for us in His humanity. God understands our human nature.

2. Lion. This is the face of authority. God welds authority over Satan, demons, angels and mankind. God is our ultimate judge. Through Jesus Christ He is our ultimate Redeemer as well, but He will judge mankind the next time He arrives. The lion is the "king of the jungle." A lion has authority. God rules and judges like a lion. So, should we as well.

3. Ox. This is the face of labor. God works to guide us, He worked to redeem us from our sins, and He will work with us to the end of the age. We as Christians are also to work in the Kingdom. The ox is a beast of burden. The ox is an animal that works a plow or carries a load. The ministry in the Kingdom is also work and a heavy load.

4. Eagle. This is the face of spirituality. Eagles are birds that soar high in the sky. They are admired that they live higher than any other creature. They are also birds of prey. Eagles have always represented Spirituality and a higher spiritual order. God dwells in a higher spiritual realm and as Christians, so should we. Eagles have been known to soar to great heights, high into the heavens. We Christians are to soar high in our spirituality in revelations, visions, prophecy, dreams, gifts of the spirit and miracles. We are to soar high in the spiritual heavens in the presence of God.

The Coming Christ: The prophecies concerning Jesus Christ which are recorded in the Old Testament may be classed under four categories.

1. King-----------Lion----PS 2:6; Is 32:1; Dan 9:25. *"Yet have I set my king upon my holy hill of Zion."*

2.   Servant--------Ox-------Is 42:1; 52:13. *"Behold my
servant..."*

3.   Son of Man---Man----Is 7:14; 9:6-7; Dan 7:13-14.
"...Behold, a virgin shall conceive, and bear a son..."

4.   Son of God---Eagle---Is 9:6-7; 40:3-9.   *"...The mighty
God..."*

The Branch: Jesus Christ is set forth in the Old Testament
as the Branch four different times and for four different reasons.

1.   The Branch--King-----Lion---Jeremiah 23:5. *"...I will
raise unto David a righteous Branch..."*

2.   The Branch--Servant--Ox-----Zech 3:8. *"...I will bring
forth my servant the BRANCH.*

3.   The Branch--Man------Man---Zech 6:12. *"...Behold the
man whose name is The BRANCH..."*

4.   The Branch--LORD---Eagle--Is 4:2. *"In that day shall
the branch of the Lord..."*

Behold: Jesus Christ is introduced four times in the Old
Testament by the word "behold."

1.   Behold, the King-----Lion---Zech 6:12. *"...Behold the
man whose name is The BRANCH..."*

2.   Behold, the Servant--Ox-----Is 42:1. *"Behold my
servant..."*

3.   Behold, the Man------Man---Zech 3:8. *"...behold, I will
bring forth my servant the BRANCH."*

4.   Behold, your God-----Eagle--Is 40:9. *"...Behold your
God!"*

The Gospels: The four Gospels reveal the four natures of God. There is but one Gospel with four presentations. Four pictures of one Christ are given. The combined Gospel records set forth a personality rather than present a connected story of a life.

1.   Matthew--Christ as King-----Lion---presented to the Jews to reveal Jesus Christ as their Messiah.

2.   Mark------Christ as Servant--Ox-----presented to the Romans to show them the practical nature of Jesus Christ.

3.   Luke------Christ as Man------Man---presented to the Greeks to reveal the Godly nature of the man, Jesus Christ.

4.   John------Christ as God-------Eagle--presented to the Church to reveal the Divine nature of Jesus Christ.

Four-Fold ministry: In Ephesians 4:11-12 we see that the Christian Church is made up of four separate ministries that work together for the growth and health of the Church.

1. Apostles. These are ministers that start new churches in non-Christian lands and strengthen existing churches. After starting new churches, they see to it that it grows. This can also include a church denomination superintendent or other Church leadership positions, since these positions deal with authority and growth into unchurched areas.

2.   Prophets.   These are church members who have prophetic gift in order to strengthen an existing church. Prophets deal with the spiritual side of ministry.

3.   Evangelists. These are ministers that travel the world and increase the faith and gain new converts for existing churches. These men and women are the hardest working members of the Church.

4. Pastors/Teachers. These are ministers or members who oversee a church. Pastors and Teachers do the same ministry.

111

These members deal with people and their problems. They minister to the human side of the Church. They teach and preach the Gospel.

1. Apostles------------Lion---Authority

2. Prophets------------Eagle--Spirituality

3. Evangelists---------Ox-----Ministry

4. Pastors/Teachers---Man---Humanity

Four-Fold Church leadership: Under the leadership of the Spirit, the apostles organized the early Church in a four-fold manner.

1. Bishops. These are male ministers who had been pastors for many years and are now a leader over several to many churches in a grouping.

2. Pastors. These are male ministers that lead a church. They are the final authority of the local church.

3. Elders. These are elder saints, men and women, who help the pastor lead a church.

4. Deacons. These are men and women in a church who deal with ministry matters within a church. These saints make the local church operate.

Full Mention Principle

The Full Mention Principle is a portion of Scripture where God speaks His mind on a certain subject. Other areas of Scripture will, and can, deal with this same subject, but God sometimes gives the full mention of a subject in one location of Scripture.

Holy **Spirit:** *Acts 2:* In the second chapter of Acts we have the Full Mention of the Holy Spirit infilling people. The key verses of these three chapters are 2:4. And 2:38-39. Other Scriptures mentioning the Holy Spirit are found in Isaiah 4:4, 28:11-12, 33:14-15, 44:3; Zephaniah 3:9; Malachi 3:3; 1 Corinthians, etc. Before, only selected people received the infilling of the Holy Spirit, but in Acts 2 we have the mass infilling of thousands of people.

Salvation: *Romans 10, 11, 12:* These three chapters of the book of Romans give us the Full Mention of salvation. The key verse of this subject is 10:9, "That if thou shalt confess with thy mouth the Lord Jesus, and shalt believe in thine heart that God hath raised him from the dead, thou shalt be saved." The plan of salvation is found in Acts 2:38, and the application of that salvation is found the rest of the book, but salvation is explained in more detail in these three chapters of Romans.

Christian **Service:** *Romans 12:* The twelfth chapter of the book of Romans gives us the Full Mention of Christian service. The key verses of this chapter are 12:4-5, the rest of the chapter explains it in more detail.

Duties *to State and People:* *Romans 13:* Paul tells the Roman Church to be obedient to the government authorities in all things, and to love people. He told them this when the government was persecuting them for being Christians.

Figure 25: God is our Potter

Judging: *Romans 14:* Paul tells us to be patient with each other's sins and shortcomings and to accept each other. He then tells us to not do anything to make younger saints fall. This is a big subject and can be found throughout the Bible, especially in the Gospels, (Luke 6: 34-49). But this chapter puts it all in a nutshell.

Immorality in the Church: 1 Corinthians 5: The city of Corinth was a port city, filled with sailors and the sinful business that surrounded this industry. Certainly, the church in this city was made up of repentant drunks, prostitutes and con men, so Paul spends an entire chapter on this subject.

Family relations: 1 Corinthians 7: In this chapter Paul writes about marriage, slavery, the singles and widows. He deals with all types of family relations which is so important.

Rights and duties of ministers: 1 Corinthians 9: The Apostle Paul teaches the church about the rights and duties of Apostles, pastors and any type of spiritual leadership.

Idolatry: 1 Corinthians 10: The Apostle Paul here deals with the practice of idolatry in the diverse Roman world in which they lived. Idolatry is still with us today; we just worship different idols. Abortion, sports, hobbies, jobs, or anything that unnecessarily takes up our time.

Spiritual gifts: 1 Corinthians 12, 14: The Apostle Paul talks about the spiritual gifts that church member receive from the Holy Spirit. Two full chapters! A healthy church will operate by the spiritual gifts of its members. It is divided by a chapter on love. This was not an accident! The active ingredient of our spiritual gifts is love.

Love: 1 Corinthians 13: The Apostle Paul teaches the church what is a Godly love. It is a blueprint for our behavior to be based on. It is sandwiched between two chapters on spiritual gifts. This was not done by accident. All spiritual gifts need to be done in love.

Resurrection: 1 Corinthians 15: The Apostle Paul teaches us about our resurrection by giving us Jesus Christ, and His resurrection as our example. As He was resurrected, so shall we be resurrected.

Christian Giving: 2 Corinthians 8, 9: The first mention of organized giving money to God is found during the building of the Tabernacle in the wilderness in Exodus 25:2. The people are told to give willingly and with a happy heart. The idea of giving happily and with a happy heart is the only requirement from God, and we see this over and over again. We see this in Exodus 35:5,21; 1 Chronicles 29:9,14; Ezra 2:68; Nehemiah 11:2. The Full Mention is of Christian giving in the New Testament is 2 Corinthians 8-9, but the key verse is 9:7, *"Every man according as he purposeth in his heart, so let him give; not grudgingly, or of necessity: for God loveth a cheerful giver."*

Christian Liberty: Galatians 5: The Apostle Paul here starts this chapter telling us that we have liberty in Jesus Christ, and the last part of the chapter Paul tells us how to achieve that liberty that is available to everyone.

Faith: Hebrews 11: The writer of the book of Hebrews wrote a large chapter on faith. In the proceeding chapter he tells us to come near to God. Then he writes his chapter on faith. Then the following chapter is who we need to have faith, God our Father.

The Tongue: James 3: The Apostle James teaches us to be careful what we say and how we say it. It is still an excellent chapter for today.

False Teachers: 2 Peter 2: The Apostle Peter teaches us what to look for in false teachers and the dangers and motivation of these people. This chapter is still very much relevant for today.

Second Advent: 2 Peter 3: The Apostle Peter gives us an entire chapter on the promise of the Lord's coming back for His Church.

God's Love: 1 John 4: All of the Apostle John's writings is a warning against Gnosticism. This chapter he teaches us to discern the false spirit of Gnosticism.

Figure 26: God's Love

God's Glory Principle

This is a principle where God will make an impossible situation just so that He can receive the glory for the outcome of that situation. God likes to showcase His Glory and Mercy as a prelude to what He would do on the Cross! The Apostle Paul understood this principle very well. He told us in Romans 9:21-23. *"Hath not the potter power over the clay...if God, willing to shew wrath, and to make his power known..."*

The Exodus: God created all of the drama of Moses going to Egypt to free the Israelite's, all of the plagues, and the hardening of pharaohs heart to make it all seem impossible until the very end. All of this was mainly done to maximize the glory for God, and show the Israelite's that He alone is their Savior.

Jericho: Joshua 6. The city of Jericho was the strongest fortress city in Palestine. The Israelite's could not take the city without heavy equipment. God told Joshua something ridicules like marching around the city seven times! All so that God could maximize the glory for Himself.

Gideon: Judges 6-8. God instructed Gideon to attack a large, trained army with a very small and untrained group just to make things impossible. God maximized the glory for Himself.

David and Goliath: 1 Samuel 17. God sent the little shepherd boy, called David to fight a large well-trained giant. It seemed impossible which maximized the glory for God.

Jehoshaphat's choir: 2 Chronicles 20:21. King Jehoshaphat was fearful when he had gotten reports of invasion from all sides. He called on the LORD for help, and God told him go to the place where the enemy would be, Moabites and Ammonites, and to just stand there! They did that, singing as they went, and God had the enemy kill themselves. God made an impossible situation in order to maximize the glory for Himself.

Nehemiah's Wall: Nehemiah 6:16. Nehemiah was sent to reconstruct the walls of the city of Jerusalem. When he saw all local political opposition and the peoples lack of will, it looked impossible. God made it so, and provided the way to maximize the glory for Himself.

Israel's Light: Isaiah 49:6. The prophet Isaiah said that Israel, and her Messiah, would be a light unto the Gentile world. This seemed impossible at the times due to the fact that Israel was in a backslide condition! But, seven-hundred years later Jesus did just that on the cross.

Grace Principle

This is where God suspends, or lays aside, His own Laws in order to show His Grace on a person or a nation. The Apostle John wrote in John 1:16-17, *"And of his fulness have all we received, and grace for grace. For the law was given by Moses, but grace and truth came by Jesus Christ."* Also, the Apostle Paul wrote in 2 Timothy 1:9, *"Who hath saved us, and called us, and called us with an holy calling, not according to our works, but according to his own purpose and grace, which was given us in Christ Jesus before the world began."*

Noah: Noah and his family lived in a wicked time. *"And God saw that the wickedness of man was great in the earth, and that every imagination of the thoughts of his heart was only evil continually."* Genesis 6:5. God set aside judgment for Noah, *"But Noah found grace in the eyes of the Lord."* Genesis 6:8.

Abraham: Abram was just an older man with no children in an average community. God showed grace to him with a promise of greatness and vast lands. God did not have to choose Abram, but he decided to show grace to him. Genesis 12.

Joseph: Joseph was an arrogant and sinful young man, but God showed him grace from the life of slavery in which he had found himself. Genesis 37.

Moses: Moses was a murderer and a sinful man, but God showed mercy and grace, to him, in the desert.

Judges: Throughout the book of Judges the people of Israel would fall into sin and God would extend grace to save them from themselves.

Rahab: Rahab was a prostitute and not worthy to receive God's grace until she helped the spy's of Israel and God extended His grace to her.

David: King David was caught up in sexual sin and then murder. The penalty for those sins is death. God, instead, after David's repentance, extended His grace to him.

Figure 27: God's Grace

Illustrative Mention Principle

This is where God shows His anger at certain kind of sins by judgment. By doing this God highlights His displeasure of those sins, but sin in general.

Disobedience: Genesis 3:14-19: Adam and Eve disobeyed the Word of God and so God had to judge them to show His displeasure and for an example to the future generations. The judgment was separation from God and the loss of security of the Garden.

Corruption and violence: Genesis 6-8: The whole world was corrupt and violent, 6:11-13. This highlighted sin was judged in Genesis 7-8. The judgment was a world- wide flood that wiped out the earth so that God could start over.

Pride: Genesis 11: Man had built a tower to walk into heaven, without an invite. Man desired to "make a name" for himself, Genesis 11:4. God judged man with their greatest fear at the time. To be "scattered abroad upon the face of the whole earth. Genesis 11:4.

Homosexuality: Genesis 18:16- 19:29: This was by far the overwhelming sin of Sodom and Gomorrah. We can see this in Genesis 19: 4-5. The judgment for this sin was death and hell fire in the form of molten sulfur. This area today has the second largest deposits of sulfur in the world!

Lack of Faith: Genesis 22: Because of Abraham's lack of faith in Chapter twenty with Abimelech, God decides to judge Abraham and to prove his faith and obedience with the sacrifice of his only son. The judgment was a severe test for Abraham to prove his faith.

Blasphemy: Leviticus 10: Nadab and Abihu, the sons of Aaron offered strange fire before the Lord. The Lord immediately judged them by a righteous fire, killing both of them! This was done as an example to illustrate the importance of service before the alter. Here, also, God shows that he will punish blasphemy most severely!

Figure 28: Christ

Literary Structure Principle

This is a principle where God, through His Bible writers, structures Scripture in an organized way to make a certain point, or communicate additional information. Literary structure is common in literature and especially in poetry. Books have been written about this subject, so I will just give a few examples of Alternation and Introverted Parallelism.

Examples of Alternation:

Joshua- 4:1-9: An alternation pattern in describing a building of a memorial to God.

A. Twelve men.

   B. Twelve stones.

      C. The place.

A. Twelve men.

   B. Twelve stones.

      C. The memorial.

A. Twelve men.

   B. Twelve stones.

      C. The place.

The Book of Jonah: The book of Jonah is a very organized writing done in an alternation fashion.

A. Calling.

    B. Disobedience.

        C. Consequences.

            D. Prayer.

                E. Deliverance.

A. Calling.

    B. Obedience.

        C. Consequences.

            D. Prayer.

                E. Correction.

Proverb 31: This proverb is written in an alternation fashion after a short introduction.

A. Her husband.

    B. Her occupation.

        C. Her Character.

            D. Her household.

                E. Herself.

A. Her husband.

    B. Her occupation.

        C. Her character.

            D. Her household.

                E. Herself.

2 Thessalonians: The Apostle Paul used alternation in forming his thoughts in his second letter to the Thessalian church. This is a very long example of alternation, so I will not write it out here, but it can be found in 2 Thessalonians 1:3-3:15.

A few other examples can be found in John 3:20-21; Matthew 23:16,17; Acts 2: 14-36; Ezekiel 36: 26,27; Jeremiah 17: 5-8; 1 Corinthians 3:6,7; Psalms 1; Isaiah 55:8-9.

Examples of Introverted Parallelism:

Isaiah 6:10: Here is a small version of introverted Parallelism.

A. Heart.

    B. Ears.

        C. Eyes.

        C. Eyes.

    B. Ears.

A. Heart

Luke 1:68-79: Here is a larger one given to us by the Apostle Luke.

A. Visitation.

    B. Salvation.

        C. Prophets.

            D. Enemies.

                E. Covenant.

                E. Oath.

            D. Enemies.

        C. Prophet.

    B. Salvation.

A. Visitation.

Other examples of Introverted Parallelism being used are in Genesis 3:19; Exodus 9:31; Numbers 15: 35,36; Deuteronomy 32:16; 1 Samuel 1:2; 2 Samuel 3:1; 1 Kings 16:22; 2 Chronicles 32:7; Psalm 8; Psalm 23; Psalm 76:1; Psalm 117; Psalm 105: 4-8; Psalm 135:15-18; Psalm 150; Proverbs 1:26,27; Proverbs 3:16; Isaiah 5:7; Isaiah 11:4; Isaiah 50:1; Isaiah 51: 8-9; Isaiah 60:1-3; Daniel 5:19; Matthew 6:24; Matthew 7:6; Romans 9: 21-23; 1 Corinthians 1:24,25; 2 Corinthians.

Okay, why is literary structure important in Biblical Hermeneutics you might ask? Well, by seeing the literary structure of a book or a letter, or even a chapter, we can see a "birds' eye" view of the text. By seeing the "big picture" of a given text we can see the context more clearly. We can observe the thought process of the author as he organized his work. This is also very helpful in understanding the context of the writing.

Metaphor Principle

Metaphor is comparison by direct assertion, in which the speaker or writer describes one thing in terms of something else. Most metaphors are designed; IE., the author intends to make a direct comparison. These can usually be identified from the metaphors are metaphors presumed to be unintentional.[11]

The Bible is filled with metaphors. It is probably the most common figure of speech used in the Bible. God used them, Jesus used them, the apostles used them. Locating metaphors and understanding how and for what they are being used is critical in the proper understanding and interpretation of the Bible.

A metaphor should not be confused with a Simile. The difference can be slight. While the Simile says, "All flesh is AS grass" (1 Peter 1:24), the metaphor carries the figure across at once, and says "All flesh IS grass" (Isaiah 60:6). This is the distinction between the two.[12]

The Simile says, "All we like sheep," while the Metaphor declares that "we are the sheep of His pasture."[13]

Let it then be clearly understood that a Metaphor is confined to a distinct affirmation that *one thing*, IS *another thing*, owing to some association or connection in the uses or effects of anything expressed or understood.[14]

For example, "All flesh IS grass." Here "flesh" is to be taken literally as the subject spoken of, and "grass" is to be taken equally literally as that which *represents* "flesh."[15]

---

[11] Mickelson, A. Berkeley. *Interpreting the Bible.* William B. Eerdmans Publishing House, Grand Rapids, MI., p. 183. 1963.

[12] Bullinger, Ethelbert William. *Figures of Speech used in the Bible.* Baker Book House, Grand Rapids, MI., p. 735. 1897.

[13] Ibid.

[14] Ibid.

[15] Ibid, p. 736.

Psalm 23- The Lord is my Shepherd: Here, we have a Metaphor; and in it a great and blessed truth is set forth by the representation of Jehovah as a Shepherd. It is He who tends his People, and does more for them than any earthly shepherd does for his sheep. All his titles and attributes are so bound up with this care that in this Psalm we have the illustration of all the Jehovah-titles:

In verse 1. "I shall not want," because He is JEHOVAH-JIREH (Genesis 22:14), and will provide.

In verse 2. "He loadeth me beside the waters of quietness, because He is JEHOVAH-SHALOM (Judges 6:24), and will give peace.

In verse 3. "He restoreth my soul," for He is JEHOVAH-ROPHECHA (Exodus 15:26), and will graciously heal.

In verse 3. He guides me "in the paths of righteousness," for He is JEHOVAH-TZIDKENU (Jeremiah 23:6), and is Himself my righteousness, and I am righteous in Him (Jeremiah 33:16).

In verse 4. In death's dark valley "Thou art with me," for thou art JEHOVAH-SHAMMAH (Ezekiel 48:35), and the LORD is there.

In verse 5. "Thou preparest a table before me in the presence of my enemies," for Thou art JEHOVAH-NISSI (Exodus 17:15), my banner, and will fight for me, while I feast.

In verse 5. "Thou anointest my head with oil," for Thou art JEHOVAH-MEKADDESCHEM (Exodus 31:13, etc.), the LORD that sanctifieth me.

In verse 6. "Surely" all these blessings are mine for time and eternity, for He is JEHOVAH-ROHI (Psalm 23:1), Jehovah my Shepherd, pledged to raise me up from the dead, and to preserve and bring me "through" the valley of death into His glorious kingdom (John 6:39).[16]

Salt- Matthew 5:13: "Ye are the salt of the earth" : I.e.., ye are (or represent) with regard to the earth what salt is to the other things, preserving it from total destruction; just as the few righteous in Sodom would have preserved that city.

Body- Matthew 26:26: "This is my body." Few passages have been more perverted than this simple metaphor. They offering at the Last Supper of bread and wine is not the body of Christ, it is just a metaphor.

Bread of life- John 6:35: *"I am the bread of life*: I.e., what bread does in supporting natural life is a representation of what Christ does in supporting and nourishing the new, Divine, spiritual life.[17]

Light of the world- John 8:12: *"I am the light of the world."* This is a beautiful metaphor. He is not a natural light but a spiritual light.

Door- John 10:9: *"I am the door"*: I.e., I am what a door is. I am the entrance to the sheepfold, and to the Father. Yes, a door, and not a flight of steps. A door, through which we pass in one movement from one side to the other.[18]

---

[16] Ibid, p. 737-738.
[17] Ibid, p. 743.
[18] Ibid.

Vine- John 15:5: *"I am the true vine."* Jesus Christ is not a vine; this is just a metaphor.

Galatians 4:24: "Which things are an allegory: for these are the two covenants."

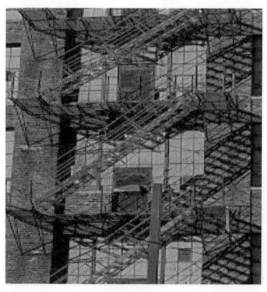

Figure 29: God's Plan

Parable Principle

In the New Testament instances of the word, it is used of a story with a hidden meaning, without pressing, in every detail, the idea of a comparison.[19]

I know of twenty-three parables in the Old Testament and forty-three in the New Testament. Because this book is not about parables, but only just this one chapter, I will only discuss two here. One parable in the Old Testament and one in the New Testament.

This likeness is generally only in some special point. One person may be like another in appearance, but not in character, and *vice versa*; so that when the resemblance or likeness is affirmed it is not to be concluded that the likeness may be pressed in all points, or extended to all particulars.[20]

For example, a lion is used as a resemblance of Christ, on account of his strength and prowess. The Devil is likened to "a lion" because of his violence and cruelty. Christ is compared to a thief, on account of his coming, being unexpected; not on account of dishonesty.[21]

The resemblance is to be sought for in the scope of the context, and in the one great truth which is presented, and the one important lesson which is taught: and not in all the minute details with which these happen to be associated.[22]

The interpretation of the parable be must further distinguished from any application which may be made of it. For example: in the Parable of the "Ten Virgins" (Matthew 25:1-12), the interpretation belongs to some special point of time immediately preceding the return of the Lord to the earth. This is

---

[19] Bullinger, Ethelbert William. *Figures of Speech used in the Bible.* Baker Book House, Grand Rapids, MI., p. 751. 1897.
[20] Ibid.
[21] Ibid, p. 751-752.
[22] Ibid.

indicated by the word "Then," with which it commences, and by its place in relation to the context. Any lesson for ourselves, as to watchfulness on our part, must come as an application of it to present circumstances.[23]

Bad Vineyard. Isaiah 5:1-7: In this parable God, through the prophet Isaiah, is telling the people of Israel that He had carefully planted them in good soil and cared for them. But they have been a bad vine and did not produce any good fruit and God is planning on pulling them up. God gave this prophetic parable just before the Babylonian captivity.

The proceeding chapter, chapter four, is about restoring Jerusalem. After this great hope then God explains His future judgment of Israel. The first half of the fifth chapter is the parable in discussion. The second half of the fifth chapter is about the evil that men do. In chapter seven we have the calling in prophecy of the Messiah. So, God gives the Jews great hope before and after this parable of judgment.

"Now will I sing to my well beloved a song of my beloved touching his vineyard. My well beloved hath a vineyard in a very fruitful hill:"

And he fenced it, and gathered out the stones thereof, and planted it with the choicest vine, and built a tower in the midst of it, and also made a wine press therein: and he looked that it should bring forth grapes, and it brought forth wild grapes.

And now, o inhabitants of Jerusalem, and men of Judah, judge, I pray you, betwixt me and my vineyard.

---

[23] Ibid.

*"What could have been done more to my vineyard,
that I have not done in it? Wherefore, when I looked that it
should bring forth grapes, brought it forth wild grapes"?*

*"And now go to; I will tell you what I will do to my
vineyard: I will take away the hedge thereof, and it shall
be eaten up; and brake down the wall thereof, and it shall
be trodden down:"*

*"And I will lay it waste: it shall not be pruned, nor
digged; but there shall come up briers and thorns: I will
also command the clouds that they rain no rain upon it."*

For the vineyard of the LORD of hosts is the house of Israel,
and the men of Judah his pleasant plant: and he looked for
judgment, but behold oppression; for righteousness, but behold a
cry.

The Two Sons- Matthew 21:28-32: This parable is
spoken by Jesus inside the Temple in Jerusalem to the chief priests
and the elders. Jesus reserved His harshest words for the self-
righteous religious people who thought they had no need for mercy!

But what think ye? A certain man had two sons; and he
came to the first, and said, son, go work today in my vineyard.

He answered and said, I will not: but afterward he repented,
and went.

And he came to the second, and said likewise. And he
answered and said, I go, sir: and went not.

Whether of them twain did the will of his father? They say
unto him, the first. Jesus saith unto them, verily I say unto you,
that the publicans and the harlots go into the kingdom of God
before you.

For John came unto you in the way of righteousness, and ye
believed him not: but the publicans and the harlots believed him:

and ye, when ye had seen it, repented not afterward, that ye might believe him.

Figure 30: Parables

Patriarch Principle

The head of a family or a community will act as the leader or Patriarch to accomplish a personal or community task Understanding a person's status is important to the story and its interpretation.

The Lord entrusted the garden of Eden to Adam because God recognized him as the Patriarch of the Garden and his future family. Likewise, Adam was held responsible for the sin of eating the forbidden fruit.

God commanded Noah to build the ark, because God recognized Noah as the Patriarch of his family.

God spoke to Abraham and gave him the promised land, because God recognized him as the family patriarch, the leader of his family.

Th female version of the Patriarch is called a Matriarch.

As far as biblical principles are compared this is a small one. But it is something to keep in mind. Family structure was very important back in those days. Today it is not as important, but we need to keep it in mind that it was everything back in those days.

Progressive Mention Principle

This is where the revelation of any given truth is increasingly clear as the Word of God proceeds to the end. The Word of God is a progression, and every progressive mention adds more details to a particular truth. The progressive mentions of different truths can be lengthy so I will just give one example.

The Coming Messiah: Little by little from the very beginning we see clues given by God of a coming Messiah.

Genesis 3:15: *"And I will put enmity between thee and the woman, and between thy seed and her seed; it shall bruise thy head, and thou shalt bruise his heel."*

When Adam and Eve brought sin into the world, God immediately gave a promise that the Seed of the woman would bruise the head of the serpent. At first a very small and vague clue.

Genesis 22: 18: *"And in thy seed shall all the nations of the earth be blessed; because thou hast obeyed my voice."*

When Isaac is born to an aging Abraham, God gives another clue. The promised Seed will be in Isaac's family linage. At first it was a promise to Eve, the mother of all humanity. Not it is narrowed down to a descendant of Isaac.

Psalm 22: *"My God, my God, why hast thy forsaken me...they pierced my hands and my feet...They part my garments among them, and cast lots upon my vesture..."*

Another clue was given to the king and prophet David in the psalm of the cross! This whole psalm is about the cross! He will be forsaken; he will be crucified, and they shall gamble for his garments!

Psalm 34:20: *"He keepeth all his bones: not one of them is broken."*

Another clue again was given to the king and prophet David that his bones would not be broken!

Isaiah 53:4-5: *"Surely he hath borne our griefs, and carried our sorrows: yet we did esteem him stricken, smitten of God, and afflicted. But he was wounded for our transgressions, he was bruised for our iniquities: the chastisement of our peace was upon him; and with his stripes we are healed."*

Another clue was given to the prophet Isaiah about the killing of the Messiah and why he died!

Daniel 9:25: *"Know therefore and understand, that from the going forth of the commandment to restore and to build Jerusalem unto the Messiah the Prince..."*

Another clue was given to the prophet Daniel. The Israelites would come out of Babylon and return to Jerusalem to build it up for the coming Messiah.

Zechariah 9:9: **"***Rejoice greatly, O daughter of Zion; shout, O daughter of Jerusalem: behold, thy King cometh unto the: he is just, and having salvation; lowly, and riding upon an ass and upon a colt the foal of an ass."*

Another clue was given to the prophet Zechariah about the Triumphant Entry of the Messiah into Jerusalem.

Zechariah 11:12: *"And I said unto them, If ye think good, give me thy price; and if not, forebear, So they weighed for my price thirty pieces of silver."*

Another clue was given again to the prophet Zechariah about the price on the Messiah's head! Thirty pieces of silver!

Malachi 3:1: *"Behold, I will send my messenger, and he shall prepare thy way before me: and the Lord, whom ye seek, shall suddenly come to his temple, even the messenger of the covenant, whom ye delight in: behold, he shall come, saith the Lord of hosts."*

Another clue was given to the prophet Malachi that a messenger would come just before the appearance of the Messiah.

Figure 31: Progressive Mention

Prophecy Principle

Much of the Bible is prophecy, about a third of it is prophetic. Basically, prophecy is history written in advance by God, through men. It is important to know where this prophecy is located and how to interpret them. Prophets serve a dual role. They speak the Word of God to people or organizations. They also speak the Word of God about the future to warn men about their sin and coming judgments. In Biblical Hermeneutics it is the later that we need to be concerned about.

Prophecy can be broken down into many different ways. Here is how I see it in Scripture and how it should be studied. The three major categories are the prophies of his Current Time, Jesus Christ, and the End Times. These three categories can have many subcategories, but I will not get into those in this writing.

Biblical prophecy is also conditional and unconditional. Conditional prophecies are fulfilled only if Israel fulfills certain conditions laid out in the prophecy. Unconditional prophecies will be fulfilled by God without conditions.

With a third of the Bible as prophecy entire books can and has been written about it. The subject is much too large to properly deal with here, so I will just give the major categories as I see it.

Prophecy about the Current Times. This is not our current time, but the current times of the prophet declaring his prophecy.

Prophecy about Jesus Christ. There are many prophetic utterances in the Old Testament about the first and second visitation of Jesus Christ. The New Testament has many utterances of the second visitation of Jesus Christ.

Prophecy about the End Times. Information about the End Times is becoming more and more important.

Figure 32: Prophecy

Repetition Principle

This is where God continually repeats certain words or phrases in order to gain our attention or to emphasis something. At these times the Bible student should listen carefully.

"**Cursed**": There are twelve curses found in Deuteronomy 27:15-26, and again seven times in Deuteronomy 28:15-19. The first are the curses on disobedience and the later are the curses of disobedience.

1. *Cursed be the man that maketh any graven or molten image...*
2. *Cursed be he that sitteth light by his father or mother...*
3. *Cursed be he that removeth his neighbor's landmark...*
4. *Cursed be he that maketh the blind to wander out of the way...*
5. *Cursed be he that perverteth the judgement of the stranger, fatherless, and widow...*
2. *Cursed be he that lieth with his father's wife...*
3. *Cursed be he that lieth with any manner of beasts...*
4. *Cursed be he that lieth with his sister...*
5. *Cursed be he that lieth with his mother-in-law...*
10. *Cursed be he that smiteth his neighbor secretly...*
11. *Cursed be he that taketh reward to slay an innocent person...*
12. *Cursed be he that confirmeth not all the words of this law to do them...*

There are six blessings in Deuteronomy 28:2-6. These blessings are immediately after the above curses.

1. *"Blessed shalt thou be in the city..."*

2. *"...and blessed shalt thou be in the field."*

3. *"Blessed shall be the fruit of thy body..."*

4. *"Blessed shall be thy basket and thy store."*

5. *"Blessed shalt thou be when thou comest in..."*

6. *"...and blessed shalt thou be when thou goest out."*

"The Lord shall:" The statement of "The Lord shall" is repeated six times in Deuteronomy 28:7-13 and again nine times in Deuteronomy 28:20-36. The first series are the blessings of obedience. The second are the consequences of disobedience.

1. *"The Lord shall cause thine enemies that rise up against thee to be smitten..."*

2. *"The Lord shall command the blessing upon thee in thy storehouses..."*

3. *"The Lord shall establish thee an holy people unto himself..."*

4. *"And the Lord shall make thee plenteous in goods..."*

5. *"The Lord shall open unto thee is good treasure..."*

6. *"And the Lord shall make thee the head and not the tail..."*

"Cursed:" Again, in 28:16-19, we have a series six of "cursed" statements. This is the second round after twelve that we had in 27:16-26. These are the curses of disobedience.

1. *"Cursed shalt thou be in the city..."*

2. *"...and cursed shalt thou be in the field."*

3. *"Cursed shall be thy basket and thy store."*

4. *"Cursed shall be the fruit of thy body..."*

5. *"Cursed shalt thou be when thou comest in...*

6. *"...and cursed shalt thou be when thou goest out."*

"The Lord shall:" In Deuteronomy 28: 20-68 we have a series of twelve "The Lord shall."

1. *"The Lord shall send upon thee cursing, vexation, and rebuke..."*

2. *"The Lord shall make the pestilence cleave unto thee..."*

3. *"The Lord shall smite thee with a consumption, and with a fever, and with an inflammation, and with an extreme burning, and with the sword, and with blasting, and with mildew..."*

4. *"The Lord shall make the rain of thy land powder and dust..."*

5. *"The Lord shall cause thee to be smitten before thine enemies..."*

6. *"The Lord will smite thee with the botch of Egypt, and with the emerods, and with the scab, and with the itch, whereof thou canst be healed."*

7. *"The Lord shall smite thee with madness, and blindness, and astonishment of heart."*

147

8. *"The Lord shall smite thee in the knees and in the legs, with a sore botch that cannot be healed, from the sole of thy foot unto the top of thy head."*

9. *"The Lord shall bring thee, and thy king which thou shalt set over thee, unto a nation which neither thou nor thy fathers have known..."*

10. *"The Lord shall bring a nation against thee from far..."*

11. *"The Lord shall scatter thee among all people..."*

12. *"The Lord shall bring thee into Egypt again..."*

"Thou shalt:" The phrase "thou shall" is repeated thirteen times in Deuteronomy 28:30-41.

1. *Thou shalt betroth a wife, and another man shall lie with her..."*

2. *"...thou shalt build an house, and thou shalt not dwell therein..."*

3. *thou shalt plant a vineyard, and shalt not gather the grapes thereof."*

4. *"...thou shalt be only oppressed and crushed always."*

5. *"...thou shalt be mad for the sight of thine eyes which thou shalt see."*

6. *"...thou shalt become an astonishment, a proverb, and a byword..."*

7. *"Thou shalt carry much seed into the field, and shalt gather but little in..."*

8. *"Thou shalt plant vineyards, and dress them, but shalt neither drink of the wine..."*

148

9. *"Thou shalt beget sons and daughters, but thou shalt not enjoy them..."*

10. *"...and thou shalt come down very low."*

11. *"He shall lead lend to thee, and thou shalt not lend to him..."*

12. *"...he shall be the head, and thou shalt be the tail."*

13. *"...thou shalt eat the fruit of thine own body..."*

"**Blessed:**" There are twenty-two beatitudes in the book of Psalms.

1. *"Blessed is the man that walketh not in the counsel of the ungodly, nor standeth in the way of sinners, nor sitteth in the seat of the scornful. (Psalm 1:1)."*

2. *"Blessed is he whose transgression is forgiven, whose sin is covered (Psalm 32:1)."*

3. *"Blessed is the man unto whom the LORD imputeth not iniquity, and in whose spirit, there is no guile (Psalm 32:2)."*

4. *"Blessed is the nation whose God is the LORD; and the people whom he hath chosen for his own inheritance (Psalm 33:12)."*

5. *"O taste and see that the LORD is good: blessed is the man that trusteth in him (Psalm 34:8)."*

6. *"Blessed is that man that maketh the LORD his trust, and respected not the proud, nor such as turn aside to lies (Psalm 40: 4)."*

7. *"Blessed is he that considereth the poor: the LORD will deliver him in time of trouble (Psalm 41:1)."*

8. *"Blessed be the LORD God of Israel from everlasting,* and to everlasting. Amen and amen (Psalm 41:13)."

9. *"Blessed be the Lord, who daily loadeth us with benefits, even the God of our salvation (Psalm 68:19)."*

10. *"Blessed be the LORD God, the God of Israel, who only doeth wondrous things (Psalm 72:18)."*

11. *"And blessed be his glorious name for ever: and let the whole earth be filled with his glory; Amen and Amen (Psalm 72:19)."*

12. *"Blessed are they that dwell in thy house: they will be still praising thee (Psalm 84:4)."*

13. *"Blessed is the man whose strength is in thee; in whose heart are the ways of them (Psalm 84:5)."*

14. *"Blessed is the people that know the joyful sound: they shall walk, O LORD, in the light of thy countenance (Psalm 89:15)."*

15. *"Blessed is the man whom thou chasteneth, O LORD, and teachest him out of thy law; (Psalm 94:12)."*

16. *"Blessed are they that keep judgment, and he that doeth righteousness at all times (Psalm 106:3)."*

17. *Blessed be the LORD God of Israel from everlasting to everlasting... (Psalm 106:48).*

18. *"Blessed be the name of the LORD from this time forth and for evermore (Psalm 113:2)."*

19. *"Blessed are the undefiled in the way, who walk in the way, who walk in the law of the LORD (Psalm 119:1)."*

20. *"Blessed are they that keep is testimonies, and that seek him with the whole heart (Psalm 119:2)."*

21. *"Blessed is every one that feareth the LORD; that walketh in his ways (Psalm 128:1)."*

22. *"Blessed be the LORD my strength, which teacheth my hands to war, and my fingers to fight (Psalm 144:1)."*

"Vanity:" This word is used thirty-six times in the book of Ecclesiastes.

"Vanity and vexation of spirit:" This phrase is used seven times in the book of Ecclesiastes.

The Six Woe's: The six woes found in Isaiah 5:8-32 speak on the judgment on Israel for its wickedness.

1. Selfish greed- v. 8-10: "Woe unto them that join house to house, that lay field to field, till there is no place, that they may be placed alone in the midst of the earth!"

2. Drunken conduct- v. 11-17: "Woe unto them that rise up early in the morning, that they may follow strong drink; that continue until night, till wine inflame them...."

3. Mockery at God's power to judge their sin- v. 18-19: "Woe unto them that draw iniquity with cords of vanity, and sin as it were with a cart rope...."

4. Distortion of God's moral standards- v. 20: "Woe unto them that call evil good, and good evil; that put darkness for light, and light for darkness; that put bitter for sweet, and sweet for bitter!"

5. Arrogance and pride- v. 21: "Woe unto them that are wise in their own eye's and prudent in their own sight!"

6. Perversion of justice- v. 22-23: "Woe unto them that are mighty to drink wine, and men of strength to mingle strong drink: Which justify the wicked for reward, and take away the righteousness of the righteous from him!

"Verily, verily:" This phrase is used seven times by John in his Gospel; 5:24, 25; 6:26,32, 47, 53; 8:34.

"**He that hath an ear, let him hear what the Spirit saith unto the churches:**" **This** phrase is repeated six times in Revelation 2 and 3. Four times in the second chapter; 2:7, 11,17,29 and twice in chapter three; 3:6, 13.

"**Fulfilled:**" This word is used frequently in the book of Matthew.

"**Kingdom:**" This word is used fifty times in the book of Matthew.

"**Kingdom of Heaven:**" This phrase is used thirty times in the book of Matthew.

"**Salvation:**" This word is used twenty-eight times in the book of Isaiah.

"**Return:**" This is used forty-seven times in the book of Jeremiah.

"**They shall know that I am God:**" This phrase is used seventy times in the book of Ezekiel.

"**Son of man:**" This phrase is used ninety times in the book of Ezekiel.

"**The word of the LORD came to me:**" This phrase is used forty-nine times in the book f Ezekiel.

"**Glory of Israel**" or "**The glory of the LORD:**" This phrase is used eleven times in the first eleven chapters of the book of Ezekiel.

"**I shall be sanctified through you:**" This phrase is used six times in the book of Ezekiel.

Second for the First Principle

In this principle God sets aside the first and establishes the second. It is sometimes called the Election Principle. This is a continuing example that all sacrifice to God is set aside for the sacrifice of the Lord Jesus Christ on the Cross. This is strictly by revelation of God Himself for the continuing of God's Purpose (Romans 9:10-12). There are many examples of this principle throughout Scripture. First among man does not mean first among God.

Cain was set aside for Abel: God set aside the offering of Cain for the offering of the second, which was Abel's. When Cain murdered his brother Abel, God set aside Cain's family, who was first, and established Abel's family, who was second.

Ham was set aside for Japheth and Shem: Ham disqualified himself by his sinful behavior on his father Noah, and was set aside for his two brothers.

The World was set aside for Noah's family: The world had grown wicked, so they were set aside for Noah's family to begin again with mankind.

Ishmael was set aside for Isaac: Ishmael was rebellious and married Canaanite women, whereas Isaac returned to his homeland to marry a woman chosen by God.

Esau was set aside for Jacob: A blind Isaac crossed his hands (Cross) and set aside Esau and blessed Jacob. The first was set aside for the second. Esau was a man of idolatry and corruption; God could not allow that to prosper. (Genesis 48:8-19).

Reuben was set aside for Judah: *"The scepter shall not depart from Judah, nor the legislator's pen from his descendants; to him nations shall submit, until the coming of Shiloh."* When to other brothers plotted to kill Joseph, Judah convinced them to save his life.

Calvary: God set aside all former sacrifices for the Sacrifice of Jesus Christ on the Cross. Mankind's relationship to God before Calvary was set aside for a new relationship that is better and more intimate.

Salvation: God has set aside the Law of Moses for salvation through faith in Jesus Christ. "Except a man be born again," The first birth is set aside for the second. The old man is to be set aside for the new man. Our old condition is to be set aside for a new condition. Mt. Sinai is set aside for Calvary.

Heaven and Earth: Today's world is filled with sin, but God will set it aside and create a new heaven and earth. (2 Peter 3:13).

Jerusalem: The Jerusalem of today will be set aside for a future new Jerusalem. The old city that is filled with sin and strife will be replaced with a holy city where peace in God will reign.

The Old Testament is set aside for the New Testament: The Old Testament tells us where man has come from and is filled with types and prophecy of the New Testament. But our spiritual life is established by the New Testament today.

Three-Fold Principle

This is one way that God sets forth truth and highlights certain points of His Truth in a Three-Fold manner. A misunderstanding of this principle has led to the false doctrine of a trinity of God's nature. This principle is actually, instead, an example of the fullness of God's Word.

Salvation: We are saved from sin in a three-fold manner. This was all accomplished at Calvary by Jesus Christ.

1. The penalty of sin. Are past has been justified by the Blood of Christ. The penalty of sin no longer applies to the Christian because Jesus Christ has laid all of our sin upon Himself, "He was wounded for our transgressions." God knows that we can never get right with God on our own; the Law of Moses has proven his for all to see. So He provided the Cross! We are saved from the wrath of God (John 3:36; Romans 1:8; 3:23).

2. The power of sin. We have the indwelling of the Holy Spirit in the present dispensation (Acts 2). God knows that we are too weak to walk with Him. The Holy Spirit can keep us free from the bondage of sin that we were once confined (Romans 7:15).

3. The presence of sin. In the future we will be transformed into the likeness of Jesus Christ. God knows that our sin-nature body is not acceptable to Him. Are immortal bodies in Glory will not be in the presence of sin that we currently live (Romans 6:23).

The Three-Fold Work of Jesus Christ: God shows man the work of Jesus Christ consistently in a three-fold way.

1. *Titus 2:11-13: "For the grace of God that bringeth salvation...Teaching us...Looking for...".* In Titus 2:11-13 we have a snapshot of the three-fold work of Jesus Christ. We can see

the Cross which is in the past. Jesus is still today teaching us to walk righteously. We also have the hope of His return.

2 Corinthians 1:10: Who delivered us...doth deliver...he will yet deliver...." In 2 Corinthians. 1:10 we have the same message but compacted into only one verse. "Who delivered us from so great a death, and doth deliver in whom we trust that he will yet deliver. "

2. 1 Thessalonians 1:3: Remembering...hope in our Lord...in the sight of God.... "In 1 Thessalonians 1:3 it is also compacted in only one verse. "Remembering without ceasing your work of faith, and labor of love, and patience of hope in our Lord Jesus Christ, in the sight of God and our Father."

Jesus' Resurrection: In order to prepare us for the coming Resurrection, Jesus raises three different people from the dead during His ministry. This is to show His followers that resurrection from the dead is indeed possible.

1. Widows son- Luke 7:11-17.

2. Ruler's daughter- Matthew 9:18-25.

3. Lazarus- John 11.

The Great Supper- Luke 14:16-24: In a Three-Fold manner this refers to the successive ministries connected with the invitations to "the great supper."

1. "A certain man" sends "his servant" to those who had been previously "bidden." This was Peter's first ministry (Acts 2-7).

2. The "master of the house" sends him again to "the streets and lanes of the city." This is Peter's second ministry (Acts 10-12).

3.   Then "the lord" send out another servant to "the highways and hedges," This is Paul's ministry to the great Gentile world (Acts 13-28).

Scripture Highlighting: It has always been a custom among man, even in American society, that if we want to emphasize something, we simply repeat it. And most commonly we repeat it three times. This is how the ancients emphasized anything they wanted to bring to attention. Today's English language we have punctuation to make our words stand out. Ancient Hebrew and Greek did not have punctuation, so the repeated a word, words, or a sentence to stress its importance. This literary technique should not be used in numerology or proving the existence of a trinity in the Godhead. It was never intended for that.

Here are some examples of the use of this technique.

1. *Isaiah 6:3.* "And one cried unto another, and said, Holy, holy, holy, is the Lord of hosts: the whole earth is full of his glory."

2. *Revelation 1:8.* "I am the Alpha and the Omega, the beginning and the ending, saith the Lord, which is, and which was, and which is to come, the Almighty."

3. *Revelation 4:8.* "And the four beasts had each of them six wings about him; and they were full of eyes within: and they rest not day and night, saying Holy, holy, holy, Lord God Almighty, which was, and is, and is to come."

4. *Revelation 22:11.* "He that is unjust, let him be unjust still: and he which is filthy, let him be filthy still: and he that is righteous, let him be righteous still: and he that is holy, let him be holy still."

5. Revelation 22:13. *"I am Alpha and Omega, the beginning and the end, the first and the last."*

God has had three relationships to man: God has dealt with mankind in three different ways. The Father, the Son, and the Holy Spirit. This is not to be confused with a trinity, which was an invention that occurred over the centuries. God has dealt with man in three separate relationships in order to do His will. There is only one God, but He has related to us in three different forms.

1. *Father.* Jesus is Yahweh. Many Old Testament statements by or about Yahweh (Jehovah) are specifically fulfilled in Jesus (Isaiah 40:3,5; 45:23; 52:6; Jeremiah 23:5-6; Zechariah 11:12; 12:10; John 8:58; Philippians 2:9-11).[24]

2. *Son.* Jesus Christ is the one God incarnate. *"In him dwelleth all the fullness of the Godhead bodily"* (Colossians 2:9). "God was in Christ, reconciling the world unto himself" (2 Corinthians 5:19). Jesus accepted Thomas's confession of Him as "my Lord and my God" (John 20:28-29). And many other Scriptural passages reveal the identity of Jesus as God. (Isaiah 7:14; 9:6; 35:4-6 with Matthew 11:1-6; Micah 5:2; Matthew 1:23; Acts 20:28; Romans 9:5; 2 Corinthians 4:4; Colossians 1:15; 1 Timothy 3:16; Titus 2:13; Hebrews 1:2; 2 Peter 1:1; 1 John 5:20).[25]

3. *Holy Spirit.* The Holy Spirit is literally the Spirit that was in Jesus Christ. "The Lord is the Spirit" (2 Corinthians 3:17, NKJV). (See also John 14:17-18; 16:7.)

The New Testament ascribes the following works both to Jesus and to the Holy Spirit: moving the prophet of old, resurrection of Christ's body, work as the Paraclete, giving of words to believers in time of persecution, intercession, sanctification, and indwelling of believers.[26]

---

[24] Bernard, David K. *The Oneness view of Jesus Christ.* Word Aflame Press, Hazelwood, MO., p. 13.
[25] Ibid, p. 12.
[26] Ibid, 13-14.

Three heavenly places: God has created three separate places. Heaven, Hell and the Earth. All three will change according to the age, but there will always be three.

1. Heaven. All parts of the Spirit realm occupied by the Angelic and the redeemed.

2. Hell. All parts of the Spirit realm occupied by Satan and demons and wicked men.

3. Earth. The physical world in which we live in today that we can touch, feel and see.

The Three-Fold "opening" that Jesus Christ gave to two disciples on the road to Emmaus:

3.   They experienced open eyes. *"And their eyes were opened, and they knew him..."* (Luke 24:31).

4.   They heard the open Scriptures. *"...and while he opened to us the scriptures?"* (Luke 24: 32).

5.   They had opened their understanding. *"Then opened he their understanding, that they might understand the scriptures,"* (Luke 24:45).

Jesus warns Peter of his three denial's: Jesus Christ at the Last Supper warns Peter that he will deny him three times before the rooster crows. *"And he said, I tell thee Peter, the cock shall not crow this day, before that thou shalt thrice deny that thou knowest me.* (Luke 22:34). This was fulfilled in verse fifty!

Peter's rejection of unclean animals: The Apostle Peter had received a vision of unclean animals on a large sheet that descended from heaven. Peter heard a voice that said to kill and eat. Peter rejected this commandment three times.

"But Peter said, not so, Lord; for I have never eaten anything that is common or unclean." (Acts 10: 14).

"And the voice spake unto him again the second time, What God hath cleansed, that call not thou common." (Acts 10:15).

"This was done thrice: and the vessel was received up again into heaven." (Acts 10: 16).

Three ethnic divisions: The Bible is a book about three different groups of people that make up the world. The Jews, Gentiles, and the Church. We must always know to whom God is addressing while studying Scripture.

1. Jew. Jewish people descendants of Abraham.

2. Gentile. All non-Jews who are not part of the Church.

3. Church. Jew and Gentile believers in Jesus Christ as the Messiah, forming one unified body.

The Revelation given to John: In order to understand the end of times and the book of Revelation we need to understand and keep in mind the Three-fold Principle. Here are some examples.

David's Son: Jesus Christ, David's Son, was to have a three-fold role.

1. Priest. He was not to be a priest like the Levites, but instead after the order of Melchizedek. David was not a priest, nor could he ever be one since he was of the tribe of Judah. Jesus Christ would be a priest, but a different kind of one, an eternal priest.

2. King. Jesus Christ is King of King and Lord of Lords.

3. God. Jesus Christ was and is God wrapped in flesh who has redeemed all of mankind.

The Three Applications of the Seven Letters: Jesus Christ told the Apostle John to write letters to the seven churches in Revelation 2-3. These letters have a threefold application.

1. They apply to the actual churches they were addressed to.

2. They apply to churches in general.

3. They have a prophetic history of the entire Church age. The Church age will last two-thousand years, from the time of Christ's crucifixion to the rapture of the Church.

The Three Roles of Jesus in Revelation: In the book of Revelation, Jesus Christ will play three different roles.

1. King. John seen Jesus Christ in heaven sitting on the throne as King of Kings and Lord of Lords. We read this in Revelation 4:2. Here God is showing us that He is ruler of the universe and is in control of all that is happening.

2. Lamb. In Revelation 5 we see Him as the Lamb slain for the sins of mankind. His purposes the Lamb was to open the seals revealing God's judgment on the world. As King sitting on the throne, or as the Lion of Judah, He cannot do this, but as the Lamb of God, slain and sacrificed as our "Passover" (1 Corinthians 5:7), He both can and does.

3. Lion. As the Lion of Judah Jesus plays the role of judge. A defender of His Jewish and Christian children. A destroyer of the wicked, and the eternal judge of Satan and all of mankind.

The Kingdom of the Son: The coming Kingdom of Jesus Christ will be set up in a three-fold way.

1. Decent. The Kingdom will begin by the descent of the Lord from heaven to the mount of Olives, splitting it in half.

2. Judgment. Jesus Christ will come the second time as judge, and He shall judge the whole world.

3. Rule. Jesus Christ will rule the entire world from New Jerusalem.

The Kingdom: The Kingdom of God here on earth will have a three-fold aspect.

1. The second coming of Jesus Christ will mark the beginning of His Kingdom on this earth. Psalms 96:9-10; 98:9.

2. He will rule over the nation of Israel, the Jews, God's chosen people. Psalm 78:8-11.

3. Jesus Christ will have rule over the entire world. Psalm 78:8-11.

Distress: In the days of Jesus, it was customary for Jews to pray the same prayer three times. A good example of this is found in Matthew 26:36-44 where Jesus was in distress and prayed three times, *"O my Father, if this cup...."*

God's Calling: God revealed to Jeremiah that God called him in a three-fold manner in Jeremiah 1:5. *"...I knew thee...I sanctified thee...I ordained thee...."*

God revealed through the apostle Paul that God calls us in a three-fold manner in Galatians 1:15-16. *"...who separated me...and called me...that I might preach Him...."*

Christian Life: Paul seems to say in Philippians 3:10-11 that there is a three-fold aspect to the Christian life. *"That I may know Him...fellowship of His sufferings...attain unto the resurrection...."* First, the learning of Christ and His Word soon after salvation. Second, enduring persecution that always follows a public conversion. Third, a hope of resurrection to heaven after death.

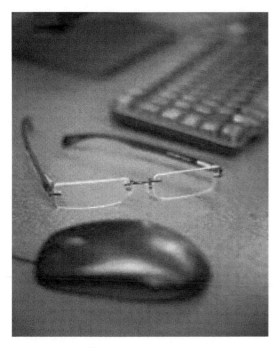

Figure 33: Three but One

Time -Gap Principle

This is where in certain verses or between verses in Scripture there is a gap in time from a few days or even up to thousands of years. If we have a long gap in time in Scripture it is important to understand that this is happening. Sometimes this time gap is mentioned, but sometimes it is not mentioned.

This principle is not to be underestimated by the Bible student; it is one demonstrated by Jesus Christ Himself in the use of Isaiah 61:1-2 in Luke 4:17-21.

Nehemiah 2:8-9*: "And a letter...And the king granted me, according to the good hand of my God upon me. Then I came to the governors beyond the river...."*

Isaiah 9:6-7: *"For unto us a child is born, unto us a son is given: and the government shall be upon his shoulder....* "The first part of verse six in about the incarnation of Jesus Christ. Then time jumps more than two-thousand years to when Jesus Christ will actually rule the earth for a thousand years on the Throne of David in the New Jerusalem. At that time the government will be upon His shoulders.

Isaiah 61:1-2: "To proclaim the acceptable year of the LORD, and the day of vengeance of our God.... "Verse one and the first half of verse two, is about Jesus Christ and his ministry here on earth. Whereas, the last part of verse two jumps ahead more than two-thousand years when Jesus shall return a second time to judge and reap vengeance on the world as He takes His saints away. So, this comma separates a gap of more than two-thousand years.

We know this because Jesus Christ Himself proclaimed this in the beginning of His ministry as recorded by Luke in his Gospel (Luke 4:16-21). Jesus reads this verse, and a half then closes the book. The rest of chapter sixty-one of Isaiah will be fulfilled later.

Daniel 9:24-27: "*...And he shall confirm the covenant with many for one week....* "*These* were not weeks of days, but of weeks of years. Of the seventy weeks of years (490 years), sixty-nine were from the seventh year of the Persian king Artaxerxes the first in 457 B.C. to the crucifixion. The last week (7 years) has to do with the restoration of Israel. Two-thousand years later this still has not happened. So, in verse twenty-six just after the Messiah is "cut off" we have a gap of about two-thousand years. We can read about this further in book of Revelation chapters ten and eleven.

Hosea 1:4. God: commanded Jehu to judge the house of Ahab for his wickedness (2 Kings 10). He did this, but he was much to severe and now God will judge the house of Jehu and cease the kingdom of Israel. From the death of Jehu and the taking of Israel by the Assyrians is about forty years. So, the last part of verse four has a forty-year gap in it.

Luke 2:40: "*And the child grew....*" This describes Jesus growing up from a baby to about twelve years old. So we have about a twelve-year time jump.

Luke 2:52: "*And Jesus increased in wisdom and stature....*" This time jump takes Jesus from about twelve years old to thirty years old, about eighteen years.

Acts 1:8: "...*ye shall be witnesses unto me both in Jerusalem and in all Judea, and in Samaria, and unto the uttermost part of the earth.* "*Here* God commands His disciples to preach to the whole world. They finally do, but this transitional period lasted about ten years before the first Gentiles were saved in Acts chapter ten.

Acts 9:6: "...*go into the city, and it shall be told thee what thou must do.* "*Jesus* tells Paul to arise and go into the city. We must realize that Paul was not outside the walls of Damascus, but he was still three-days from the city. There is a three-day gap in time before the story picks up and Paul is healed.

Acts 9:23: "*And after that many days were fulfilled.* "*Three* years passed between 9:22-23. This event is recorded in Galatians 1:15-18 and also in Second Corinthians 11:32-33. While Luke did not record it, he did leave room for it.

Acts 9:43: "...*he tarried many days in Joppa....* "*Peter* did not return to Lydda, but stayed in Joppa possibly as long as one year.

Acts 11:26: "...*a whole year....* " We should understand that this one verse spans one year of time.

Acts 13-14: This first missionary journey reads very fast, but we should keep in mind it lasted about two years!

Acts 14:28: "*And there they abode long time with the disciples.* " Between missionary journeys they stayed the city of Antioch in Syria and ministered for quite some time, maybe several years. During this delay the conference in Jerusalem in chapter fifteen takes place.

Acts 15:36-18:22: This second missionary journey of Paul, which was much more extensive than the first one, spanned a period of three to four years.

Acts 18:11: *"...a year and six months....* "This verse is important; it tells us that Paul was in this city for a year and a half. This was a long time just in this one city. If we read the book of Acts to quickly it will seem as if Paul is just moving along, but he did not constantly move, but did make long stops to teach.

Acts 18:23: *"And after he had spent some time there...."* There is a gap in time when Paul rests and ministers in Antioch in Syria. Most scholars seem to agree Paul stayed about three years in Antioch during this time.

Acts 18:23-21:16: This third missionary journey was Paul's longest trip and probably lasted about four to five years.

Acts 19:8-10: *"...three months...."* Paul spent three whole months in just one synagogue preaching Christ before he was forced to leave. *"...space of two years...* "In verse ten we see that Paul did not leave the city but instead preached in the school of Tyrannus daily for two more years. Church history says that the Ephesians worked in the morning and did their resting from eleven in the morning to four in the afternoon. Paul probably preached during this time.

1 Peter 1:10-11: "*...searching what, or what manner of time...* "*The* prophets of old did not understand that the Messiah would humble Himself on the cross to provide God's grace we enjoy today. They did not understand there would be a gap of more than two-thousand years until fulfillment.

Figure 34: Time Gaps

Typical Principle

This is a divinely appointed illustration of a spiritual truth. The Greek word has the meaning of an impression or stamp, mark, pattern, form, or mold. A Type is a person or object that will be a pattern for a person or object in the near or distant future.

There is no such thing as a perfect type. By their very nature they are not perfect. A type is like a shadow, we can see an outline of our body on a sunny day, but there are no details. A type is a shadow of the future fact. The type must have a genuine resemblance to the point that it is obvious.[27]

Types are prophetic symbols. They are a fusion of the temporal and the eternal, the Old and the New. So, to have any hope of understanding them, we must have rules to find them in the text and to properly interpret them. Rules for their interpretation are then:

1. Commence with a thorough New Testament study and find out what it teaches on typology. This is the absolute starting point in any work on typology.

2. From the study of the New Testament locate the great typical areas of the Old Testament.

3. Locate in any given type the typical and the accidental. What is typical will be guided by the study of the New Testament which will indicate especially what sort of things are typical, and what areas are typical in the Old Testament. Therefore, the good interpreter will refrain from pressing his interpretation into too much detail, realizing that in any type there is a dissimilar element.

---

[27] Davidson, Andrew Bruce. *Old Testament Prophecy.* T & T Clark, Edinburgh, Scotland., p. 210. 1905.

4. Keep within the bounds of good sense. There is the temptation to suggest a new interpretation for the sheer sake of its novelty.

5. Do not prove doctrine from types unless there is clear New Testament authority. Hebrews very plainly proves theology from types, but we may not do the same since we are not inspired. Types, for the most part, illustrate truth. The central rod of the construction of the wall of the tabernacle proper cannot be used to prove the unity or security of the believer, but it may be used to illustrate the same.

6. Clothe your interpretations with humility. What is clearly taught in the New Testament may be asserted with confidence, but beyond that humility should clothe our efforts. Typology is a kind of double-sense interpretation, and in all double-sense interpretation there is the two-fold danger of going beyond the evidence of Scripture, and of the unbridled use of the imagination. Humility must be our spirit in those territories that cannot be treated with the finesse of literal exegesis. To do otherwise is to obscure the Word of God.[28]

There are six kinds of symbols that are Typical:

1. Persons may be as typical as Adam, the federal head of a race; Abraham, the pioneer of by-faith justification; Elijah, the prefigurement of John the Baptist; Joseph, the rejected kinsman, yet future savior; David, the great king; Solomon, the chosen son; and Zerubbabel, the head of a new society.

2. Institutions: The sacrifices look forward to the cross, the Sabbath to the salvation rest, the Passover to redemption, and the theocracy to the coming kingdom. 3. *Offices:* The Old Testament offices of prophet, priest, and king are all typical of Christ, who is prophet, priest, and king.

---

[28] Ramm, Bernard. *Protestant Biblical Interpretation.* W. A. Wilde Company, Boston, MA., p. 146-147. 1950.

4. Events: The exodus is a pattern of deliverance, and the wilderness journey has many events of typical significance.

5. Actions: The lifting up of the brazen serpent is a type of the crucifixion, and the ministry of the high priest on the day of atonement is typical.

6. Things: The ark of the tabernacle is a type of the incarnation; the incense a type of prayer; and the curtains express principles of access to God.[29]

As you can clearly see there are many types in Scripture. There are so many that a entire book could easily be written on them. I will only give a few examples here in this chapter so that you can get a basic idea of them. Not only do we have six different typical symbols, but we have innated and inferred types as well.

An innate type is one that has been mentioned in the New Testament. The inspired Word of God has declared it a type. An example of an innate type would be the brazen serpent that was lifted up by Moses in the wilderness. Jesus said that He would be lifted up so that all men could have eternal life (John 3:14-15; 12:32). There are many others.

An inferred type is one that is not specifically mentioned in the New Testament, but is justified as a type by the New Testament and historical references that line up to the rules of Typology. We are allowed this by the fact that Jesus Himself commanded us to search out the Scriptures (Old Testament) because they spoke about Him (John 5:39-44). The most popular inferred type is Joseph being a type of Christ. There are many others, and as you read and study Scripture, try to find them.

Here I will give some of my personnel favorite types found in God's Word. You will see how they enlighten the Bible stories.[30]

---

[29] Ibid, p. 147.
[30] Philips, John. *Bible Explorers Guide.* Kregel Publications, Grand Rapids, MI., p. 110-111. 1987.

Joseph as a Type of Christ: This is an inferred Type. To begin with he (Joseph) was the father's well-beloved son. He was set apart from his brethren, his kinsmen according to the flesh, by his coat of many colors, the garb of a chieftain or a priest. His brothers envied him and could not speak peaceably to him. They resented his favored relationship with the father. His dreams, which spoke of his coming glory and power, moved them to murderous rage. When his father sent him to his brothers, they conspired against him and sold him for the price of a slave. Handed thus over to the Gentiles, he was falsely accused and made to suffer for sins not his own.

In the person of Pharaoh, he "preached" to others who were there awaiting their final sentence. For the chief butler he had a message of life; for the chief baker he had a message of a second and worse death. Brought out of prison, Joseph was given a position second only to that of Pharaoh, exalted to the right hand of majesty, and thus became a ruler in the land of Egypt before whom everyone would bow.

Exalted -- taken from obscurity and raised up to share his place on high -- Joseph was given a Gentile bride, and thereafter began to deal faithfully with his natural brethren, the children of Israel. He brought them to the place where, in deep contrition, they confessed their long rejection of him. Finally, "all nations" came to him.

Antiochus Epiphanes as a Type of the anti-Christ-Daniel 8:9: This is an inferred type. The "little horn" in Daniel 8 is a Type of the future anti-Christ. "This 'little horn' is correctly identified with Antiochus Epiphanes (175-164 B.C.) .... There is common agreement on this identification, because this man brought extreme suffering on the Jews in Palestine. This suffering was of a nature corresponding to the descriptions, of atrocities

174

wrought by this 'little horn.' Antiochus Epiphanes wanted to force the Jews to become Grecian in their thinking and practices, especially in matters of religion. He had spent time in Athens, prior to becoming king of Syria, and apparently had become enamored with the Grecian way of life. He wanted the Jews to change their Mosaic practices and devised laws to this end. When the people resisted, they were made to suffer, with large numbers paying with their lives. The Temple was desecrated and the alter and/or statue of Zeus Olympius was erected, later referred to by Christ as the 'abomination of desolation' (Matthew 24:15).

In view of these matters, the reason Daniel used the same term, 'little horn,' for this man of ancient history as for the Antichrist of the future becomes discernable. The later little horn will be like the earlier little horn in bringing suffering on the Jews. Antiochus did this to a degree much greater than any other person of ancient time; the Antichrist will do the same to a degree much greater than any other person of future time. He was, then, a kind of antichrist of ancient time, and, therefore, appropriately called by the same term. The use of this term thus had a prophetic function. By designating this person of history as the antichrist of ancient time, Daniel was predicting the character and deeds of the Antichrist of future time. Those who would live after the period of Antiochus Epiphanes could know the general pattern of the final Antichrist by studying the life of the former one.

Thus, we can learn the following information about the Antichrist. He will have the same interest as Antiochus Epiphanes in changing the religious beliefs and practices of the Jews. This is also suggested by his causing 'the sacrifice and the oblation to cease' at the Temple, as noted in Daniel 9:27. He will carry out this interest to the extent of employing great force, even to the slaughter of all who oppose him. And he will desecrate the Temple (which will have been restored at least by the midpoint of the tribulation)

175

through the erection of another 'abomination of desolation' (Daniel 9:27; Matthew 24:15).[31]

Figure 35: Christ, our Passover Lamb

The Passover Lamb: This is an innate type "...For even Christ our Passover is sacrificed for us." (1 Corinthians 5:7). This is typical of Christ, and it is divinely authorized. This takes us back to Exodus 12. It is a most remarkable chapter and contains one of the most astounding types of the Bible. Israel is in Egypt and in bondage. Here we have the judgment on the land, and the deliverance of Israel by the Passover Lamb. That night Israel was led out of bondage.

From Exodus 12 we go to John 19:36. "A bone of him shall not be broken." John the Baptist had it revealed to him that Christ was the lamb. No one is ever called the Lamb of God except Christ,

> *"The next day John seeth Jesus coming unto him, and saith, Behold the Lamb of God, which taketh away the sin of the world." (John 1:29).*

[31] Wood, Leon J. *The Bible and Future Events.* Zondervan Publishing House, Grand Rapids, MI., p. 101-102. 1973.

God never had in mind any lamb saves the one Lamb. In spite of slaying of thousands of lambs, you never read of Passover lambs, but *"the Passover Lamb."* On the night of the Passover, there were possibly thousands of lambs slain, but God did not say "Kill them," but, "Kill it." All divine sacrifices are embodied *only* in the Lamb slain from the foundation of the world. Calvary culminates, down to the minutest detail, the slaughter of innumerable lambs. [32]

One thing that stands out in Exodus 12 is the fact that Israel was in bondage, in slavery. Their burdens had become so great that they were almost unbearable, *"...and the children of Israel sighed by reason of the bondage..."* (Exodus 2:23). They were in sin. We are inclined to think of these people as martyrs, but they deserved just what they endured. They were not only slaves, but also sinners as well. They were as sinful as the Egyptians; in fact, they were worse than the Egyptians, for they had light that the Egyptians did not have. They had contact with God and had such promises and enlightenment as the Egyptians had never had. Israel was worshiping the gods of the Egyptians, *"ye pollute yourself with all your idols..."* (Ezekiel 20:27-32). Israel was so contaminated, and so headstrong in her idolatry, that God thought to destroy her. This is a picture of man outside of Christ.

They were delivered through the Lamb. It was God's purpose to bring these people out of Egypt, to deliver them. But, before He could set them free, before they could know the blessing of Jehovah dwelling in their midst, before they could walk with God, the sin question must be taken care of.

God will not associate Himself with sin; God is Holy. It was God's plan to deliver them after the question of their sin was settled. God settled that question by passing the sentence of death

---

[32] Ibid.

against the first-born in the land of Egypt, *"And all the firstborn in the land of Egypt shall die…"* (Exodus 11:4-5). That included the firstborn in the Hebrew homes as well as the firstborn in the homes of the Egyptians. God brought the judgments against the gods of the Egyptians, and so against those who worshiped the gods. God singled out in every case, the household's pride, the firstborn, the heir of the family, the one in whom the hopes of the house were centered. This firstborn is representative of the family and of the family's guilt. The whole family is under condemnation that rests upon Jew and Gentile. *"All have sinned,"* and *"The wages of sin is death."* That is what Christ received on the cross, the wages of sin. They were wages He had not earned, because He was sinless; but He received them anyway.

The condition then, is this: Here is a people, sinful slaves under condemnation. When God said, "I am will come down to deliver them," that is grace. Moses was not going to deliver them, but was merely an instrument in the hands of God. God was the Deliverer. Another Deliverer came 1900 years ago; Christ, the same *"I AM,"* came down to deliver men, that is grace. God came down, incarnate in Christ, in order that slaves might be delivered. What has been said concerning the people of Israel is true of man today, "…There is none righteous, no, not one…" (Romans 3). There is no difference. All have not committed the same kind or the same number of sins, but all have sinned. There was no difference between Israel and Egypt, but God put a difference between them, there was the lamb between.

One lamb is always sufficient, and Christ is always sufficient. The lamb must be a perfect specimen, a firstborn male, without outer defilement and inner wrong, (1 Peter 1:19; Hebrews 7:26). The lamb must be slain. A live lamb would not save the firstborn in the home. The blood must be sprinkled on the two sides and above the door. Something must be done with the blood. Some

178

say that if Jesus died for the world, the world must be saved. They forget that the blood must be applied. It takes more than the shedding of blood to save a sinner. There must be a personal appropriation. The blood must be put on the door in the form of a cross. Christ living cannot save. *"Except the Son of Man to be lifted up,"* (John 3:14).

Blood in the Lamb-Incarnation

Blood in the basin- Death

Blood on the door- Application

The lamb must be put into the fire. It not only had to be slain, but it also had to be roasted as well. There might be some crosspieces to hold the limbs apart. Thus, the lamb was literally crucified. This gives us a picture of Christ crucified. He was hung before the open fire of God's wrath, and the flames of God's wrath enveloped Him.

It must not be eaten raw. The carcass had to endure the fire until the roasting was complete or until the action of the fire was complete. Christ said, "It is finished." He had endured it all. The lamb must not be soaked with water, because water would resist the action of the fire. Nothing was to be done to alleviate the sufferings of Christ on the cross.

They were to eat the lamb. The eating of the lamb would strengthen them for their journey. There are Christians today who haven't feed on the lamb, and so have not strength to get out of the land of Egypt. What was left must be burned. If any of the flesh of the lamb was not eaten, it would spoil and decay, and become corrupt. But this lamb is typical of Christ, and anything that savors of corruption must be destroyed.

Concerning the blood. The blood was sprinkled for God. It was for God's eye, not for the eye of the firstborn. The blood spilt on Calvary we have never seen, but God saw it.

179

Result of the Passover. When the Passover was over, there was death in every home in the land of Egypt. In the homes of the Egyptians it was the death of the firstborn. In the homes of the Israelite's it was the death of the firstborn lamb. There was a firstborn death in every home.

Figure 36: Lambs

The feast of unleavened bread (Exodus 12:15). This was instituted also. They were to put leaven out of their homes, and for seven days were to eat unleavened bread.

The time of the Passover. The lamb was slain at three o'clock in the afternoon; judgment came at midnight. Between three and midnight there was time for the sprinkling of blood, but after midnight no blood could be sprinkled; it was too late. Christ was crucified 1900 years ago. That was at three in the afternoon. There is a midnight of God's judgment coming, but before that time men must come under the blood, to be saved.

The New Year. In Exodus 12 we read that God changed the calendar of the Israelite's. They were at the beginning of the seventh month, but God changed it to the first month. Six is the number of man, failure and sin. Six months had passed, and the seventh had come, and the seventh was to be the new beginning based on the Passover. The old six is blotted out.

Figure 37: Offerings

The Offerings or Sacrifices- Leviticus 1:5: There are five of them: Burnt, meat, peace, sin, and trespass. It takes all five to present Christ's work. The first three are sweet savior. The last two are non-sweet savior; they have to do with sin- that is, they picture Christ as the sinner's substitute.

Types of sacrifices used. There were three kinds of four-footed beasts- oxen, sheep, and goats. There also were two birds of sacrifice- turtledoves and young pigeons.

All sacrifices were either such as were offered on the ground of communication with God (Burnt and Peace), or else they were intended to restore that communication when it had been dimmed (Sin and Trespass).[33]

The burnt offering- Leviticus 1: Entire surrender unto God whether of the individual or the congregation. Thus, it could not be offered without the shedding of blood. This portrays our Lord's perfect submission to the Father. He was obedient unto death. The sacrifice was always a male animal- indicating strength and energy. The blood was sprinkled on the alter. The animal was cut in pieces and wholly burned. Through Christ's finished work we come into the presence of God for worship. Man is unworthy and needs to be identified with a Worthy One.

The meat offering- Leviticus 2: Really a meal offering since there is no flesh in it. It comes from the vegetable kingdom. No blood. It brings before us the products of the soil- that which represents the sweat of man's brow and labor. There are three varieties of the sacrifice, and all speak of Christ. The meat offering is human perfection. It speaks of His unblemished manhood. Man, fallen and depraved, needs a substitute.

Fine flour. Ground and sifted. Speaks of evenness and balance of Christ. No excess or lack of any quality. The grain, ground between the millstones and exposed to fire, speaks of Christ's sacrifice. Frankincense. Frank means whiteness and speaks of purity. Incense speaks of prayer- "He ever liveth to make intercession." The fragrance speaks of the fragrance of His life. He is the lily of the Valley.

Baked loaves. They are cakes mixed with oil. No leaven permitted. No decay or corruption in our Lord. No honey. Honey is a natural sweetness which stands for natural sweetness apart from grace. Honey causes and promotes fermentation. Salt was to be used, preserving against corruption.

---

[33] Ibid.

Green corn. Dried by fire and beaten, pictures suffering of Christ. Full ears- excellence and perfection. The first fruits of the harvest. The best, full, first, and finest ears.

The peace offering- Leviticus 3: It speaks of a happy fellowship. It followed other feasts. It was either public or private. It could be male or female. Leviticus 7 tells us that the "inwards" were waved before the Lord, along with "the breast" and "right shoulder." The purpose of the waving was to present the sacrifice to the Lord and then receive it back to Him. This offering is typical of Christ in relation to the believer's peace. Colossians 1:20. Christ is our peace. Man has a heart alienated from God and needs reconciliation.

The sin offering- Leviticus 4: Not like the trespass offering, which only atoned for one special offense. The sin offering symbolized general redemption. This is the most important of all sacrifices. Every spot of blood from a sin offering on a garment conveyed defilement. Christ was made sin for us. Man is a sinner and needs atoning sacrifice.

The trespass offering- Leviticus 5: It provided for certain transgressions committed through ignorance. Demands confession. It was prescribed in the cases of healed lepers- Leviticus 14:12. Blood was thrown on the corners of the alters. The trespass offering shown how Christ would settle the question of sin; confession then the application of the blood of Christ. Man is a guilty transgressor and needs forgiveness.

The High Priest and his Garments: This is all found in Exodus 28.

The High Priest: Apart from the High Priest the tabernacle would be inaccessible. He was the mediator between God and man. There are two lines of priesthood: Aaron and Melchizedek. Aaron was a type or contrast. Aaron was a priest on earth: Christ never was a priest on earth. Aaron ceased to be a priest when he died;

Christ never ceases to be a priest. The work of the High Priest didn't begin until after the death of the sacrifice took place. The priesthood had to do with Israel- God's own people. All believers are in heaven in Christ. Christ is our confessor in heaven. The priesthood was on behalf of the people. Christ our Righteousness is in heaven. There is finality to His work.

Figure 38: High Priest

The garments of the High Priest: They were made of purple, scarlet, fine linen, gold, and precious stones. They were holy garments for glory and beauty- God designed. There was a coat with a long skirt and fine linen breeches. The breeches were undergarments that reached from the loins to the thigh. They speak of righteousness and purity. Aaron needed cleansing. The anti-type needed one. There was a linen girdle. This is not the girdle of the ephod. It was wound around the body. It is a symbol of service- Phil. 2:7; John 13:4- servant. After regeneration there is

184

need of daily cleansing. The robes of the ephod were blue from shoulder to the feet. One piece woven without seam. There was a habergeon with two holes for arms, and one for the head. The skirt was trimmed with pomegranates and embroidered in blue, purple, and scarlet. There were pomegranates and bells on the hems. Blue was the heavenly color showing the heavenly character of His ministry. Bells speak of the tongue, showing the perfect speech of the Son of God. The bells speak of testimony. Pomegranates speak of fruitfulness- fruit of many seeds. Whenever there is testimony there is fruit. Whenever the priest went into the Holy of Holies, the people could hear the bells and so knew he was alive. How do we know Jesus lives in heaven? Because of the bells. On the day of Pentecost, there was a fulfillment of the ringing of the bells. Bells and pomegranates are never separated. Whenever there is testimony you find a fruitfulness of the Spirit.

Ephod. It was an outer garment made of blue, purple, scarlet, fine-twined linen and gold. They were joined with gold. There was an onyx-stone on each shoulder. On each stone were the names of the six tribes of Israel. The typical significance is that He bore all Israel on His shoulder before God. So, Christ bears us before God. The shoulder is the place of strength.

Breastplate: It is of the same material as the ephod. It is foursquare. There were twelve stones for the twelve tribes, on the breast. The High Priest bore them on his heart as well as on his shoulder. The typical significance is we are always in the place of affection.

Mitre: It is the head covering and shows obedience toward God.

Golden plate: It was the crowning piece. It was fastened to the mitre with laces of blue. On it was "Holiness to the Lord." Our holiness is in the presence of God.

185

Urim and Thummim: For wisdom. God spoke to His people through these. Probably they were two precious stones carried in the pouch of the breastplate. The words are Hebrew words meaning lights and perfection.

Figure 39: Priests

Principle of Weeks

The Bible revels a unique time system called "Weeks." This time system exists nowhere else in human history. There is a total of five different kinds of weeks.

The Week of Days: Genesis 1:1- 2:3 The week of Days is found in the creative week where God creates the universe and the earth and all of the life on the earth. This is where God created the universe in six days and rested on the seventh day. A week of Days.

The Week of Weeks: Leviticus 23:9-22. The week of weeks is seven weeks from the Feasts of the First Fruits to the Feast of Pentecost.

The Week of Months: The feasts cycle is located in Leviticus 23:1-44. It is a seven-month cycle of feasts unto the Lord.

The Week of Years. *If thou buy an Hebrew servant, six years he shall serve and in the seventh he shall go out free for nothing, Exodus 21:2. Six years thou shalt sow thy field, and six years thou shalt prune thy vineyard, and gather in the fruit thereof; But in the seventh year shall be a sabbath of rest unto the land, a sabbath for the Lord: thou shalt neither sow thy field, nor prune the vineyard.*

The Week of Millenniums: From the beginning of mankind to the end of mankind should be seven thousand years. A week of Millenniums. We see this example in the book of Daniel 9: 24-27.

Conclusion

If we open the Word of God blindly, we will end up tripping and falling. That's when we misinterpret Scripture! We can start from the beginning and read till the end and get something from it. But as you can see from this humble book, the Bible is no ordinary writing! The Bible needs to be broken up into pieces and studied differently. God has designed it specifically to be studied and discussed among man.

As to most things, there are rules that must be followed for the sake of coercion and organization. The Bible is no different in that respect. It must be studied in an organized manner and adhering to these hermeneutical rules will make God's Word come alive with vibrancy.

Other books, written by man, speak to the mind. The Bible is a book written by God through men, and it speaks to the mind and soul. Prophecy found in the Bible proves that it was written by God. No other book can claim its prophetic record. The Bible has always been in a position to liberate man from the oppression of man, and his manmade religions, that always tends to enslave men. It is truly a book of the ages specifically written for the enlightenment of the soul of mankind.

William James Roop, M.A.B.S.

Bibliography

Bernard, David K. *The Oneness view of Jesus Christ.* Word Aflame Press, Hazelwood, MO.

Bullinger, Ethelbert William. *Figures of Speech used in the Bible,* Baker Book House, Grand Rapids, MI. 1897.

Davidson, Andrew Bruce. *Old Testament Prophecy,* T & T Clark, Edinburgh, Scotland. 1905.

Hartill, J. Edwin, *Principles of Biblical Hermeneutics,* Zondervan Publishing House, Grand Rapids, MI. 1947.

Mickelson, A. Berkeley, *Interpreting the Bible,* William. B. Eerdmans Publishing Company, Grand Rapids, MI. 1963.

Phillips, John, *Bible Explorers Guide,* Kregel Publications, Grand Rapids, MI. 1987.

Ramm, Bernard, *Protestant Biblical Interpretation,* W.A. Wilde Company, Boston, MA. 1950.

Virkler, Henry A. *Hermeneutics: Principles and Processes of Biblical Interpretation.* Baker Book House, Grand Rapids, MI. 1981.

Wood, Leon J., *The Bible & Future Events,* Zondervan Publishing House, Grand Rapids, MI. 1973.

Notes

Notes

Notes

Made in the USA
Middletown, DE
18 October 2022

12889267R00116